D1593657

As it had in high school and as a Navy SEAL, his strong-looking physique—augmented significantly by his wit and bluster—enabled him to grow popular, to "get over" as they say in pro wrestling parlance. "He was well below average as a wrestler," says Meltzer, recalling one particularly uninspired bout Jesse had with Moondog Mayne, a skilled wrestler. "That match was pretty bad," Meltzer says. Still, Jesse "was one of the better personalities." Taking a page from "Superstar" Billy Graham's book, Jesse would do his homework on each city, researching the local sports teams and any issue he could use to antagonize the crowd.

On the road, Jesse would try to avoid temptation whenever possible. While his fellow wrestlers would go out drinking after an event, Jesse would keep away from barroom troubles, locking himself in his hotel room, calling Terry every night, and maintaining the discipline he'd learned in SEAL training.

"He stayed in his hotel room," Sharkey says. And when he was wrestling in Minneapolis, instead of having a beer with the fellas, "he'd just go straight home. He wanted to be with Terry. A lot of guys in the wrestling business, they go down the toilet, and get involved in drugs and drinking, but he never did."

—From BODY SLAM

BODY SLAM

THE JESSE VENTURA STORY

JAKE TAPPER

St. Martin's Paperbacks

BODY SLAM

Copyright © 1999 by Jake Tapper.

Cover photograph credits:
Top photograph © AP/Wide World Photos.
Bottom photograph © Eric Miller/Liaison.

ISBN: 0-312-97202-4

Printed in the United States of America

St. Martin's Paperbacks edition / May 1999

10 9 8 7 6 5 4 3 2 1

Acknowledgments

This book could never have come about without the faith, guidance, leadership, and friendship of my agents, Neal Bascomb and Christy Fletcher. I am immeasurably grateful to them for believing in me and working tirelessly on my behalf. I should also sing the praises of Joe Veltre, my editor at St. Martin's Press, and his assistant Erika Fad. Joe, in particular, merits some of the credit for this book: the whole thing was kind of his idea.

Writers seldom get to thank people who've helped them throughout the years. As even the most famous writers toil in relative obscurity, we tend not to have stock speeches "thanking the Academy" filed away. Therefore, "Acknowledgment" sections of books are handy in expressing our gratefulness to those people who helped us achieve, as modest as those achivements may be. There are a number of individuals whom I need to thank, including David Talbot and Joan Walsh at *Salon Magazine*; David Carr and Erik Wemple at *Washington City Paper*; Glenn Frankel, Joel Garreau, Peggy Hackman and Rose Jacobius at the *Washington Post*; Guy Raz and Ellen Weiss at National Public Radio; Alex Heard at the *New York Times*; Josh Cohen at *George*; Maggie Murphy, George Blooston, Doug Brod, and Anna Holmes of *Entertainment Weekly*; David Eggers of *Timothy McSweeney's Internet Tendency* acclaim; Ana Marie Cox from *Mother Jones*; Stacy Mason, Susan Glasser, Craig Winneker, Tim Burger, Lee Horwich and Ed Henry at *Roll Call*; Bill Thomas and Lynda Robinson at *Captial Style*; Eliot Kaplan at *Philadelphia Magazine*; Jay Heindrichs, Jim Collins, and Theresa D'Orsi at the *Dartmouth Alumni Magazine*; Andrew O'Hehir at *Swing*; Lance Gould at *Spy*; Steve Friedman and Lee Smith at *GQ*; and lastly, the inimitable Joey Anuff of *suck.com*. A special thanks to Marjorie Margolies-Mezvinsky, Jody Powell, Professors Maury Rapf and John Michael Hayes, Jim and Sarah Brady, and Tony Auth.

Thanks also to: Weiss, Flug, Rake, Daryl, Haber, Scully, Corny, Pace, Barts, Fred, Gabby, Groq, McKenna, Sean, Brett, Caroline, Brad, Feinstein, Amy, Bob, Schrader, Rusty, Brett & Jen, Karp and E.T. Cohen. I'm lucky to have a wonderful family, all of whom assuredly know how I feel about them already, but as long as I'm listing people I'm fond of, I might as well give the names of those I love the most: Grammie and Grampie, the Chang Gang, Shelly, Lisi, Becky, Debby, and Mom and Dad.

And of, course, my brother Aaron, to whom this book is dedicated.

About the research methods

As Governor Ventura signed a six-figure deal with a separate publisher for his autobiography, he refused to cooperate with repeated interview requests. The information contained herein comes from hundreds of hours conducting dozens of interviews with Governor Ventura's present and former colleagues, friends, teachers, fellow soldiers, opponents (in both wrestling and politics), and reporters. I thank those individuals for their time. I am indebted to the exemplary reporting by the outstanding Minnesota press corps—particularly Minnesota Public Radio, the Minneapolis *Star Tribune*, Brooklyn Park *Sun Post*, and St. Paul *Pioneer Press*. I have tried to either reference or footnote those Jesse Ventura quotes which were taken from exclusive interviews.

INTRODUCTION

Tom Brokaw winced.

Here it was, one of the most interesting election nights in recent memory—a night where Democrats nationwide were upsetting all pundits' predictions, an evening whose abysmal GOP performance would end up felling House Speaker Newt Gingrich, an ephemeral moment of jubilation for the beleaguered President Bill Clinton—and yet, in the midst of all this . . . this *history,* this *gravitas* . . . the internationally known and respected anchorman found himself talking via satellite to a . . . a . . . a former pro wrestler.

Appearing bemused more than anything else, Brokaw briefed the television public as to the events leading to this ignominious interview: Out in Minnesota that night, November 3, 1998, Reform Party candidate Jesse "The Body" Ventura, forty-seven, had eked out a plurality victory in a three-way race for governor. Though 63% of the state's voting public had pulled levers for other candidates, 37% was good enough for that night, as it had been a three-way race. January, 1999, would bring Governor Jesse "The Body" Ventura to the state capital in St. Paul.

Brokaw's apparent discomfort may have been understandable. This new governor was a man, after all, who had once dressed in oversized sunglasses and a feather boa, taunting opponents named Brutus "The Barber" Beefcake and George "The Animal" Steele. He was a man whose Hollywood film career was so, well, so modest, that his last role—Arkham Asylum guard in the 1997 dud *Batman and Robin*—garnered him thirty-seventh listing in the credits, and didn't even earn the dignity of a name. A candidate whom First Lady Hillary Clinton had derided as a circus sideshow only days before . . . *this* was the next governor from the state of statesmen? From the land that begot senators and vice presidents Hubert Humphrey and Walter Mondale, as well as Supreme Court justices Warren Burger and Harry Blackmun? *Governor* Jesse "The Body" Ventura?!

He looked funny—six-feet-five, 270 pounds, head shaved to the skull, a *Great Santini* mustache. He talked funny—like he had a ball of phlegm in the back of his throat that he just couldn't swallow. He had so much energy coursing through his veins, so much unbridled testosterone, he was constantly shaking his head palsylike, fidgeting like a nine-year-old whose Ritalin prescription had run dry. When he tried to use big words or leadership phrases to sound "gubernatorial"—"At this point in time," for instance—the result was often that he sounded like an uneducated man throwing out a phrase he'd caught on PBS while channel-surfing to *Jerry Springer*.

"Should we call you Governor Ventura or Governor 'The Body'?" Brokaw lamely joked. But Jesse couldn't hear the anchorman above the clamor of his celebration party at the Minneapolis racetrack Canterbury Park. Jesse wedged the earpiece tighter into his ear and asked Brokaw to repeat the question.

"I wanted to know whether we call you Governor Ventura or Governor The Body?" Brokaw repeated, exacerbating everything awkward about the moment—

the anchor's weak attempt at humor, the utter unpreparedness of the network for the satellite hook-up, the not-ready-for-prime-time feel of the governor, despite his serious suit.

Jesse's response was perhaps even less reassuring.

"I've actually changed that moniker. I'm no longer 'The Body,' I'm Jesse 'The Mind' Ventura," he explained, since he no longer made his living from his brawn, but from his brain.

Up until that point, Jesse had built a life and reputation that stood for a lot of things, but intelligence was hardly one of them. His body came in handy as high school swim team captain, as a member of the elite Navy SEALs during the Vietnam War, as a bar bouncer and a professional wrestler. His charisma and charm aided with the wrestling, and helped him segue toward careers in film and sports announcing and as a talk-radio "shock jock." But, truth be told, *Jesse's* mind wasn't necessarily the first thing that came to yours when his name was mentioned.

Still, as Brokaw bid Governor-elect Jesse "The Mind" Ventura adieu, and coverage of the quirky, once-quixotic man expanded to the cover of *Time,* and David Letterman's Top Ten List, it was difficult to deny that there was something attractive about Jesse. He spoke plainly, admitting his ignorance when appropriate, talking simply and honestly—*anti*-politically, even—about various issues. And always with a genuine Mih-ne-SOH-dah twang. He shunned contributions from big-money influence-accruing PACs. He was conditioning coach for a local high school football team. He seemed like a regular guy, and in interviews he gave regular-guy answers.

So beyond the wrestling glitter and Hollywood cash, past the machismo that lingered from his days as a Navy SEAL and the remnants of his egomaniacal pro wrestling persona, there was something utterly honest about the man. Something clearly not slick or packaged, a quality quintissentially un-feigned, a bluntness that bordered on crass, but in an utterly forgivable—lovable—way. Something very un-political, quite un-focus-group-tested. Something very un-Clintonian.

And yet, like the President whose intern foibles Governor-elect Jesse would mock only a few days later, on *The Tonight Show with Jay Leno,* Ventura is an enigmatic man fraught with ambition. His journey from humble beginnings to the seat of power—specifically from the south side of Minneapolis to the Governor's Mansion—took a somewhat different turn than the President's journey, and the two couldn't be more opposite in manner and style. But the story of how Jesse "The Body" Ventura ended up heading up a state that is run to the tune of $12 billion a year and employs 48,000 people is, like Clinton's own, compelling story, the tale of how one man learned how to re-invent himself, and in doing so, tap into a powerful political spirit and come to stand for something far more important than just his own ambition.

PART ONE

ONE

JIM

Bernice Lenz was just a farm girl from Independence, Iowa, but she was also a woman of incredible inner strength. Whether surviving the Depression as one of a litter of kids subsisting on oatmeal more often than not, or by getting into and putting herself through nursing school, each time the headstrong Bernice surpassed an obstacle, she would find and gun for another. Born in 1918, Bernice graduated from nursing school at Milwaukee Lutheran Hospital in 1940, and immediately enlisted in the Army. She served in Europe and North Africa during World War II, and was commissioned as a first lieutenant.

George Janos, the grandson of Czechoslovakian immigrants, endured a tough childhood as well, in the coal towns of Pennsylvania. Born in 1908, he also enlisted in the Army—at the maximum age one could do so, thirty-six. He also served in North Africa during the war, slogging through seven major battles and four years of hell. He was a sergeant, part of the crew of a tank destroyer, fighting in the infantry under General George Patton.

Though they were both in Africa during the war, their stars didn't cross until they got to Minnesota. When the war ended, Bernice moved to the Twin Cities of Minneapolis and St. Paul to study at the University of Minnesota to become a nurse anesthetist. She was an educated woman, but that year, 1945, she met and fell in love with George, who had little more than an eighth-grade education.

He had the gruff manner of a sergeant, while she retained her stern officer's bearing. Tall and muscular, George was ruggedly handsome—he had broad features, a long chin, thick nose and lustrous brown hair. Bernice was more refined, prim, and somewhere in the neighborhood of pretty. Her smile bunched her cheeks together at the corners of her mouth, and people were always noticing her legs. George was ten years older than she. When he wanted to get under her skin, he would call his stubborn wife "the lieutenant." They were married in 1946.

Bernice and George moved to South Minneapolis, into a modest two-story home. It was a lower middle-class urban neighborhood, about 100% white, with nearly as high a percentage of Scandinavians. It was, in fact, called "Swede Town."

George got a job as a laborer for the city's streets department. His friends called him "Sneakers," or "Sneaks." Because of a traumatic incident during the war, he never, ever drove—he walked to and from work each day. Bernice worked at a number of hospitals, eventually becoming chief nurse anesthetist at North Memorial Medical Center. "She was quite stubborn," says Bill Ritter, who worked with Bernice at North Memorial Medical Center and knew her for thirty-four years. "She didn't let anything stand in her way."

They started a family almost immediately. In January, 1948, they had a baby boy, who they named Jan. On July 15, 1951, they had another boy—James

George Janos, whom they called Jim. Twenty-five years later, he would go by an altogether different name—Jesse "The Body" Ventura—but in South Minneapolis back then, he was just Jim.

They were great kids, but very different in temperament. Jan was hard-working, quiet, reserved. His room was immaculate. He was intense and introspective.

However much he looked up to his brother, Jim was his opposite. He was a mischievous scamp, always getting into trouble. He was a slob and didn't work very hard in school. A jug-eared kid with a bowl haircut and brown hair, Jim was entirely devoted to his mom, though his natural playfulness would cause his parents some problems.

"I thank a higher being that my son wasn't me," Jim would later say, after becoming a father himself. "And I feel bad for my mom and dad, because I caused way more problems than my son has ever caused me."[1]

Bernice and George were strict and strong parents who demanded character from their children. When Jan and Jim stole seed packets from a local market, Bernice and George found out and scolded them pretty harshly. But however much they insisted that their children obey the rules, they never shorted them on love. "The boys were uppermost as far as she was concerned," says Ritter.

And they never shorted their kids on fun. Jim and Jan would fish for carp in the Mississippi River. Many Minnesotans have cabins by one of the state's many lakes, and the Janos family would retreat to theirs on weekends. Jan and Jim snuck into Minnehaha Academy football games.

Pro wrestling was a big deal in the Twin Cities back

then, and the brothers would listen to bouts on the
radio. They loved it. At Cooper Elementary School
one day, at the age of eight or nine, Jim was asked
what he wanted to be when he grew up. He said a pro
wrestler.

"That's a ridiculous idea, Jim. Go sit down," the
teacher said.

But Jim loved the sport, knew the holds and moves
and surprised his fellow grade-school opponents
whenever his gym class would pair off and wrestle.
An average student, the sleepy-eyed, slightly goofy-
looking kid would come alive in athletics. He graduated from the ninth grade at Sanford Middle School in
1966.

Bernice ran the family. She did more than her share
of the disciplining, and made sure that Jim and Jan
were on time, polite, and as studious as she could in-
spire them to be. She mothered everyone who came
in contact with her. If you saw her knitting socks or a
sweater, and you commented on how nice her needle-
work was, next time you saw her odds were she had
a sweater waiting for you. At North Memorial Hospital, her maternal instincts earned her the nickname
"Ma."

She also handled the family's finances, balancing
the checkbook and keeping track of the family's ac-
counts. Memories of the Depression cast a long
shadow—she never bought on credit, thought it was
irresponsible. Mom was the source of allowance: Once
they were old enough to drive, Jan and Jim would pop
over to North Memorial to bum a few bucks from their
mom.

George and Bernice weren't married as kids, and
they didn't live as kids, either. Bernice worked full-
time, and she and her husband, while enjoying a strong

marriage, had lives independent of one another. George retired while Bernice was still working, and he spent much of his retirement at their lake cottage.

George Janos would lead the family in discussions about politics. Minnesotans are unusually political, and George's lack of formal education didn't hold him back from offering opinions and railing against politicians. "George was a really, really nice guy. You could sit down and talk to him for hours about anything but politics," says Ritter. "You never wanted to discuss politics with George, 'cause George just had nothing but disgust for politicians." He thought they were skunks. Richard Nixon was the worst of them, he thought—a tail-less rat.

Jim's dad "was fun to be around," recalls one of Jim's friends from high school, Steve "Nelse" Nelson. "He'd sound off a lot about politicians and how they were all crooked. . . . You could hear him yelling about some politician after a news broadcast, how he was crooked."

"What's wrong with your dad?" Nelse asked once, hearing a commotion from the living room.

"Oh, he's spouting off about some politician," Jim replied. "You know George."

He had a real feel for the underdog, George Janos. "Probably in the back of his mind, Jim thinks he better not goof this up because he's going to have someone to answer to," Nelse says today.

Jim and Nelse attended Minneapolis Roosevelt High School on Twenty-eighth Avenue, home of the Teddys. It was a two-story brick building that took up a city block; its student body was urban, blue-collar, almost entirely white. "We didn't have desegregation yet," says Fred Meyer, principal of Roosevelt, who first arrived at the school in 1970. "So we had a very small number of students of color. . . . It was mainly Scandinavian, with some German.'' Freeman ''Mac'' McInroy, the now-retired end coach for the football team, as well as a social studies teacher, says that around that time the football team had ''four Andersons, five Hansons, and five or six Johnsons.''

Jim, still an average student, continued to be far more interested in athletics and his social life than he was in his studies. Clean-shaven, lean and muscular, with a full head of brown hair like his dad and a developing cleft in his chin, Jim threw himself into his extrovert persona. A popular and occasionally rowdy kid, Jim walked the halls of Roosevelt with a mischievous glint in his eyes. He went to dances, hung with his buddies, rah-rahed at pep rallies, and pitched in with charity work at the YMCA across the street.

He liked attention. Sartorially, Jim had a flair for being a little different. He'd see an outfit or style on television or in a magazine and would run downtown to buy something like it.

''One year, he was wearing this real ridiculous shirt,'' Nelse recalls. ''This Errol Flynn shirt with puffy sleeves, and it was flared.

''I said, 'Jim, I can't believe you're wearing this.'

''He said, 'What's wrong with it?'—He was baiting me. . . . He enjoyed being the center of attention.''

Though Jim was popular, he didn't really seem to have one clique of friends with whom he was especially close. He was more like the guy whom everybody was friends with, whom everybody wanted to pal around with. He seemed to have a good sense of self— he was one of those few kids in high school who seems to have it all together. A handsome dude whose build got more than a few looks—he was voted ''Best Physique'' in his yearbook—Jim dated a lot of girls, but there was never anyone special. Just a lot of running around and having fun.

Occasionally, it was clear that Jim might be more than just a beer-drinking, skirt-chasing, rabble-rousing high school jock. One time an unbelievably inane debate broke out—the kind of bureaucratic proposal that makes high school sometimes seem like purgatory. There was a movement to make one of the staircases "up" and the other "down." Since they were on opposite ends of the building, a lot of the students thought that seemed unreasonably time-consuming. *Who thinks of these things?* they said.

Jim was one of the students who took a leadership role in winning a majority of both sides to agree to a compromise: The stairways would remain open to both "up" and "down" traffic, but everybody would stay to the right. Problem solved.

A leader. His senior year, as captain of the swim team, he led the Teddys to a 6–3 record. He was the best swimmer on the team by far, the only one who competed in the state tournament that year. In the 1969 yearbook, Jim stands as clearly the largest guy in the team photo. Six-foot-two, 190 pounds, Jim was lean but had big and defined lats, biceps, and pecs. He had to for his swimming specialty, which was the exhausting butterfly stroke.

"He always seemed happy and goal-directed," says Gary Fortier, an assistant swim coach at the time. "He was Mr. Reliable." Whenever they needed anyone to fill in for another swimmer, Jim—the team star—would gladly volunteer for the task. "When we got in a bind we could always rely on him—he'd take care of it for us," Fortier says.

Though his grades were fairly underwhelming, there was one class that interested him: "Mac" Mc-

Inroy's eleventh grade history class. "Contrary to what some people thought, he was a very sharp individual," Mac says. Jim was always an active participant in class discussions, always very opinionated about the issues of the day, very much his father's son.

Sometimes the debates would get so heated they'd almost get ugly. McInroy recalls Jim almost coming to blows with his fellow end on the football team, John Folta, over a local civic debate. The baseball diamonds and grass around the local lake—Nokomis—were regularly littered with beer cans. So a local alderman had been drafting legislation to fine anyone caught littering. Folta's dad owned a local bar, and Folta was worried that the bill would affect his father's business. But Jim was "a conservationist even way back then," according to Mac, and he got to arguing with Folta.

"We've got to protect things," Jim said, according to Mac. "We can't have it messed around."

But Folta disagreed. *What was the big deal?*

And, as was a pattern in Mr. McInroy's history class, Jim would seldom back off when challenged. It became heated.

"Finally, I said, 'Listen guys, if you don't like something, don't just sit there and'—excuse the French—'bitch about it,' " Mac recalls. " 'Get your name on a petition and do something about it.' "

Mac was always telling the kids that. America was a country where individuals could make a difference. If you didn't like something, you could propose an initiative, write a referendum, try to recall an elected official or a law. He would say it over, and over, and over again over the course of his thirty years of teaching at Roosevelt. Get involved. Run for office. Play a role. He never knew if anyone was listening.

TWO

JANOS THE DIRTY

The Janos boys were supposed to go to college. That was the plan, anyway.

But, influenced by a Richard Widmark movie called *The Frogmen* and, whimsically enough, an aquatic childhood toy, Jan had joined the Navy when he graduated in '66. He'd even signed up for the elite SEALs division.

During Jim's Christmas vacation, Jan returned to Minneapolis and made quite an impression on Nelse. Jan had gotten through SEALs training and already done a tour at Da Nang.

"He was well-tanned and muscled, and he had a shaved head," Nelse recalls.

"What the hell did you do, Jan?" Nelse asked.

Jan told Nelse all about the Navy, the SEALs, Hell Week. Nelse had been thinking about going to Mankato State, but didn't have the time, motivation, or money for school. Nelse thought he belonged in Vietnam.

That was the kind of neighborhood South Minneapolis was. Fairly untouched by the peace movement, Swede Town was suffused with "a lot of patriotism, regard for country and the good old U.S. of A," according to Roosevelt principal Meyer, who served in 'Nam himself. "The young men in the area were more apt to serve in the military than they were not to serve," Meyer says.

Nelse had been researching various military options, and the SEALs kept popping up as a possibility. SEALs sounded great—it was the best of the best, real manly stuff. But Jan tried to talk him out of it. He wanted Nelse—and Jim, for that matter—to go to college and have fun.

Teachers at Roosevelt were preaching the gospel according to Nixon: the U.S. belonged in Vietnam, they said, our boys needed to be in Vietnam to stop Communism. George Janos didn't buy it—he hated Nixon to begin with, and he suspected that somebody was just making money off the whole deal. Jim, influenced by the domino theory taught at school, disagreed. They had typically heated Janos dinner-table debates on the subject.

If either of his sons were going to join up, George wanted them to sign with either the Navy or the Air Force, so they could learn a trade. "[T]he Army or the Marine Corps would only teach us how to pound gravel with our feet,"[2] Jim would later recall.

Immediately after graduation, Jim had started working for the state highway department, repairing bridges. When his supervisor found out that Jim was only seventeen, he told him to hit the road and come back on his eighteenth birthday that July. He did and was re-hired.

In September, Nelse told Jim he was going to go down to the Navy recruiters.

"I want to do what your brother's doing," Nelse said.

Jim tried to talk him out of it. Hadn't he listened to what Jan had told him? But Nelse's mind was decided.

There'd been talk of Jim soon heading off to Northern Illinois for school on a swimming scholarship. That's what his dad wanted. That's what the family had decided. But later that day, Jim phoned up Nelse.

He'd come with him, Jim told Nelse. Just to hear what the recruiter had to say—nothing more. But when they had finished, on September 11, 1969, the Navy SEALs had two new recruits.

Jim went home and looked at himself in the mirror. "What the fuck did I do?" he asked himself.[3]

"I didn't plan to enlist," Jim later recalled. "But they're like car salesmen. They're recruiters. That's their job. I got down there, signed on the line, and got the military ID."[4]

There was a lot more to it than that, of course. Despite their day-and-night differences in personality, Jim looked up to his older brother Jan quite a bit. Even though Jan was shy and introverted—"the complete opposite of his brother," according to Nelse—he had an inner strength and confidence that Jim admired.

"In his own way he is stronger than I am," Jim once said.[5] So Jim would follow Jan to Coronado, California, just south of San Diego, to try and become a SEAL.

Jim and Nelse had signed up under deferred enlistment, so they had a few months to raise some hell and relax before the tough days began. Jim returned to the highway department for a spell so he could earn just enough to survive until the day he was to report to boot camp. He didn't want to have a nickel on him when he arrived.

They reported for boot camp on January 5, 1970. The physical challenges of boot camp were no big deal for the two high school jocks. But Jim began to have second thoughts once he was first presented with the tenor of military training.

They were "standing with a bunch of other fresh recruits being chewed out by this little shit," Jim would later recall. Jim turned to Nelse.

"Steve," he said, "you're lucky I don't kill you right now. We could be back home chasing women and having a good time. Instead here we are standing under this fucking hut being yelled at and we haven't done anything."[6]

Soon boot camp was over and Jim and Nelse passed the SEALs screening tests. But there was an initial problem with Jim's training testing. SEALs recruits can't be colorblind, and Jim was. A flag was put on his application.

His mom got on the case. She called Senator Hubert Humphrey's office. The Minneapolis recruiter had told Jim that his color-blindness wouldn't be a problem, she told one of the Senator's aides.

Jan got to work on the problem, too. He talked to a few people.

Soon Jim was told he could take the test again. He failed thirteen out of fourteen questions. But the test proctor reported that Jim had gotten them all right. Jim wondered what happened. Later, he found out that the test proctor had been stationed with Jan overseas.

It was President John F. Kennedy's love of military strategizing that officially created the SEALs. Kennedy had ordered that all branches of the military were to assemble special teams to conduct clandestine, unconventional, and counter-guerrilla warfare. The Navy's response was to commission its first two SEAL—standing for Sea-Air-Land—teams, in January, 1962.

The SEAL program had its roots in the group of

Navy sailors who'd been selected to clear obstacles from Utah and Omaha beaches in Normandy and southern France in preparation for the American invasion, in 1943. These groups were then consolidated for underwater demolition work in the Pacific during World War II. Similar squads—or Underwater Demolition Teams (UDTs)—continued these operations during the Korean War. Then Kennedy bestowed upon them the honor of officially being the Navy's best of the best.

It's nearly impossible to get through even basic training: BUD/S (Basic Underwater Demolition/ SEAL) Training boasts an 80% dropout rate.

It's easy to see why. The first phase of training is an insanely intense program of physical conditioning that in 1969 lasted six weeks, and has since been increased to nine. Students run in boots, through obstacle courses and slog through mud; they swim up to two miles in the Pacific Ocean; they are constantly being pushed to the very brink of their physical capabilities. In the final part of Phase One, Hell Week, from Sunday until Friday, students get a total of four hours of sleep—and never in more than forty-five-minute increments. The demands of SEALs training make the most aerobicized men and women in your gym look as active as a tree sloth.

"Hooyah!" the drill sergeant yells.

"Hooyah!" return the recruits.

It takes a ball-breaker almost beyond human comprehension to push SEAL students through Phase One. Jim's instructor at BUD/S, in fact, Terry "Mother" Moy remains to this day one of the scariest people Jim has ever met.

"My job was to get them used to discomfort," Moy says. In his four years as a SEAL instructor, Moy saw

about 2,300 students come through the front door.
"They didn't all leave out the back door, though," he
says. Of those 2,300, he says he only can recall about
a dozen. Jim Janos is one of them.

"His brother had come through before him," Moy
says. Jan "was a good student. We didn't have any
problems with him."

Jim was a different story.

It's not that Jim wasn't a good recruit—he was.
And, as Moy points out, "he had the pressure of his
brother being through" which "he handled . . . quite
well."

But Jim was a wiseass. Which is to say nothing
more than he had a good sense of humor. But in military training, having a sense of humor—as well as a
strong sense of self—can also paint a target on the
back of your fatigues.

A sense of humor "leaves you open to a little
play," Moy says, " 'cause the instructors have a sense
of humor, too."

On the first day of training, Mother Moy set them
through an obstacle course that eventually they would
have to be able to complete in about ten minutes. It
took Jim almost forty-five.

Torn blisters dangled from his hands. Moy came
over to the men and asked if any of them had "flap-
pers." Jim said that he did.

"Like a lot of us, Jim was somewhat naive about
what to expect," says Tim Keeney, Jim's swim buddy
during Phase One of SEAL training. "None of us really knew what was going to happen to us. They play
with your mind a lot."

Moy told Jim to hold out his right hand. He ripped
the loose skin from it. Then he told him to rip the
loose skin from his left hand himself.

Hooyah!

Jim asked for it sometimes. The idea was to not stand out, but that was tough for him.

Once, "Mother" Moy took his students out to the Mud Flats. This was a swampy mess of land where the trainees would be made to compete and slog around for two full days. "You get them used to being dirty, cold, and tired," Moy says. "Crawling in the mud is very fatiguing. At first, it looks like fun, but hours later it's not fun—it's trying and cold."

On the first day at the Mud Flats, Jim approached "Mother" Moy, who was surveying the scene from up on a dune. In his hands Jim was holding a live mudfish—three inches long and bug-eyed.

"I found a fish," Jim said.

"You did, huh?" Moy replied. "You have a fishing license?"

Jim didn't know where this train was headed, but he knew he wasn't going to like where it let him off.

"Uh . . . no," Jim said.

"Then you'd better eat it," Moy said.

So Jim tucked the mudfish into his mouth and he swallowed it.

Alive? Moy is asked, years later.

"Of course," he replies. "What, am I going to cook it for him?"

"The fact that he crawled up there to one of the instructors showed courage and humor," Moy says.

Jim was "always quite amusing," says Paul Spark, a friend from SEAL training. "But they got on everybody's case—the idea was to make you quit. If you couldn't keep putting out, then you weren't their kind of material." SEAL training consisted of excruciating challenges that pushed you to find physical and emotional strength you had yet to tap into. If you didn't have it in you, you'd quit, which is what they wanted.

For "Mother" Moy, a twenty-three-year Navy veteran, whose four years as a SEAL instructor are the highlight of his career, it doesn't matter what success Jim achieves. He may have been a good student and a great swimmer, and if you press him on it, "Mother" Moy might even admit to being a little proud of how far his former student has come. But there is little that can alter the instructor-student dynamic of military training.

"To me, he's still a maggot," Moy says. Hooyah!

When he had fins on, Keeney was roughly as good a swimmer as Jim, so he became his swim buddy at BUD/S training. They swam together in the Pacific, for unreal lengths of time, staying no farther than five or so feet apart.

"You tend to fade at different times," Keeney says. He and Jim kept each other awake. As a team they scored the best time for an event that had the two underwater, swimming through obstacles, setting up demolitions while holding their breath.

One night Jim proved a most useful swim buddy. They were scuba diving through a San Diego bay compass course, fifteen or twenty feet under water, when Keeney inhaled the chemical supposed to take CO_2 out of the exhalant.

Keeney choked. He struggled. He started to fade.

Jim pulled Keeney up to the surface by his life jacket. They got into an observation boat nearby.

"We kept a pretty close eye on each other," Keeney says.

Seven weeks of Second Phase followed. Then nine of Third.

Second Phase continued the physical demands of First Phase, but speed and endurance were pushed even further. New instructors took over and taught students how to scuba dive. Even for recreational divers who scuba for sport, scuba can be a dangerous endeavor. For SEALs, who are taught to scuba for great distances and with little compressed air, it's even worse.

In Third Phase, Jim learned all about demolitions, reconnaissance, and land warfare. Again, instructors continued to heat up the burners on physical training. But that was nothing compared to the deadliness of explosives and the risks of rappelling, which were also part of Phase Three. And after these two phases were completed, in November, 1970, Jim and the few remaining BUD/S trainees were shuttled off to Army Airborne School in Fort Benning, Georgia, for three weeks of parachute training, which Jim completed on December 9, 1970.

Sky-diving was especially fearsome for Jim, as he was afraid of heights. He says that one of the reasons he joined the SEALs was to erase this phobia from his psyche.

One time Jim almost died. He prefers not to go into it, except to say that he accepted death as he thought it was headed straight for him.

His training class had been taken east of San Diego, where they were engaged in a practice mission to demolish a bridge. While crossing a dam, Jim—along with six others—lost his footing and fell into the turbulent water and was swept through a pipe. He was caught and tossed around. Loaded with full equipment, as he landed in the water at the other side of the dam he was weighed down as if tied to an anchor. He sank.

He didn't know which way was up. He was under water so long he started to black out.

His lungs burned as if flames were tearing through them.

He saw his parents looking down at him.

At the last second his head popped up and he sucked in a breath of air.

"It was very calm and I fully had made the decision that this was it, that I was going to die," he says today.[7]

But he ducked the Reaper and before long he graduated. Knowing that Jan had done it before him helped. "(T)hat was how I made it through training—how could I come home, and my parents would say, 'Gee, well, Jan made it and you didn't,' " he says.[8]

SEAL training was the most difficult thing he's ever had to do. Next to it, nothing else has even remotely been a challenge. "I was never the same after training," he's said. "Because then you truly know who you are down inside . . . No matter what I do now, that is the scale, that is the measuring stick. And no matter what adversities I face in life, I always go back to training and I say, 'This is nothing compared to that.' "[9]

After finishing BUD/S, Jim was convinced that there was very little he could not accomplish. "No matter how big the obstacle (is), it can be overcome," he told one reporter. "Failure, when you have the motivation, is very limited."

Jim Janos graduated from SEALs Class 58. His rating was E-4, Storekeeper third class, U.S. Navy.

"Hoo-yah!" he cried.

From completion of his BUD/S training at the end of 1970 until his last day on active duty on December 10, 1973, Jim Janos spent approximately seventeen months abroad. SEALs would rotate on foreign tours in six month shifts, after which they'd return to Coronado. At various times he served in Okinowa, Guam, Thailand, and Hong Kong.

But for much of his time abroad he was stationed in the Philippines, at Subic Bay—adjacent the city of Olongapo and off the South China Sea.

Wherever he went, his fellow SEALs differentiated between him and his older brother by bestowing upon them Viking-like nicknames that said it all. Jan was "Janos the Clean," while his little brother Jim was "Janos the Dirty."

While Jim "was a good sailor he was not a really neat person as far as uniform went," recalls his former executive officer, Captain Larry Bailey, who knew Jim in Coronado and was his executive officer in Subic Bay. "He didn't put a premium on spit-shinning his boots or making sure his uniform was neatly pressed."

But it wasn't just the crease in his fatigues—Jim's personality factored into the nickname "Janos the Dirty," too. Just as they had been as kids, Jim and Jan were noticeably opposites. Jan was lean and quietly intense, keeping to himself. In Coronado and especially in Subic Bay, in the Philippines, where he was stationed for some of the Vietnam War, Jim was not.

One of the leaders of a group of rowdy SEALs, Jim grew a Fu Manchu mustache and beard, wore an Australian bushman's hat and necklace of shark's teeth, and started lifting weights. He and his pals were a tight-knit and wild bunch.

"He had an impish sense of humor," Bailey recalls. "And he was always doing stuff to see the reactions of other people. . . . He showed up one day with his head shaven, for example. It wasn't illegal, but it was outlandish. . . . And it wasn't five days later when about a half dozen guys showed up with *their* heads shaved. . . . He was just a natural leader. People wanted to mimic him.''

Every war has its Sin Cities, suffused with brothels, drinking, gambling, and fighting, and during the Vietnam War, Olongapo was the Sin City of the Western Pacific. ''There was plenty of trouble to get into,'' says Sam Lerner, a former SEALs assistant platoon commander from that era. (Lerner's still on-duty so he asked for a pseudonym.) ''I remember Janos arriving in Subic Bay,'' he says. ''He looked like he thought he had just arrived in the Promised Land.'' And it was a promised land, Lerner says, if you were looking for ''cheap beer and a lot of girls and warm water.''

''They all looked like a bunch of frito banditos,'' Lerner remembers. ''They were these twenty-year-old kids with scraggly beards trying to look like pirates.'' It was a look and attitude they pursued even up to risking insubordination. One time, around March, 1971, as part of their amphibious exercises around the Philippines, Jim and his platoon boarded a ship of straight-laced Marines who were shocked at the SEALs' unshaven demeanor. ''So they went down below and shaved their heads—but they kept their beards,'' Lerner recalls.

Jim loved Subic Bay, thrived in it. There weren't the ridiculous rules, the minutia of the official Navy in Coronado. It didn't matter if your shirt was tucked in—or if you were even wearing a shirt—as long as you did your job and did it well. He started lifting weights and bulking up. He took martial arts instruction from a local Filipino man. The different UDTs faced off in athletic bouts. Once he even got to beat ''Mother'' Moy—who had ceased being an instructor and joined UDT-11—in a tug-of-war.

He was aggressive. Then Lieutenant Bruce Dyer,

who replaced Bailey as the UDT's executive officer midway through 1971, remembers a time that Janos the Dirty confronted him on an issue he took to be of great importance.

"I personally took input and then rewrote all the evaluations of the officers and the enlisted men," Dyer says. Generally, Dyer thought Jim a decent if unspectacular sailor. "He was just another one of the 125 enlisted guys in the team," Dyer—who was Jim's executive officer from '71 through '73—says. "I don't think he really stood out except for his size and his large personality . . . He was just an average-to-good Navy frog man."

But Dyer wanted to get across Jim's uniqueness in the evaluation. "I had written his evaluation and I was looking for the *mot juste* to describe him," he says. He settled on "truculent."

Some time later, Dyer heard that Jim needed to see him about his evaluation. "He came to my door and knocked—with a little louder knock than was probably needed—and he has a pretty deep voice then, too, and I heard, 'XO! [executive office] PERMISSION TO COME IN, SIR!' "

Dyer, curious, gave him permission.

Abiding by protocol, Jim took off his hat and entered the room.

"Sir?" he asked Dyer. "What's this word here? *'Trussalent'?!*"

"You mean *'truculent'*?" Dyer asked, amused, realizing that Jim thought it was an insult. "Jim, it means 'fierce.' "

"It took him a couple seconds, but then a big shit-eating grin came across his face," Dyer recalls. "Then he realized that I'd paid him a huge compliment. Not only had whatever confrontation he thought was going to take place not taken place, but his XO thought he was a fierce guy.'' Jim's mood brightened immeasurably.

''Of course,'' Dyer adds, ''he could have looked it up in the dictionary—but he had to come and see the XO.'' That was just the way Jim did things.

For instance, during one tedious spell in Coronado between deployments, Jim thought up a plan to return overseas—and spend much of the time there playing football. Much of the fighting was over by that time, and to boost morale, the Navy had created its own football league overseas.

Even then Jim had a gift for self-promotion and an almost shameless sense of possibility. He'd been beefing up a lot, and he thought he had what it took to maybe be a professional football player after the war. Jim approached Dyer and ''put in a request that he be allowed for his part of the tour to go over a little bit early so he could play football, in addition to his daily duties, for the Navy team in Subic,'' Dyer recalls. ''Since it didn't interfere with the performance of his duties, I said, 'Yeah, OK.' ''

''It was not a usual type of request,'' Dyer says. It showed an unusual aggressiveness. After Jim convinced all the other appropriate superior officers of the various reasons he used to justify his reassignment, Jim spent two and a half months in Subic Bay practicing and playing football. ''That was some of the best duty I ever pulled,'' he would later say. ''There was even enough time for me to go into town a time or two.''[10]

Olongapo. Sin City. The Promised Land. Jim had a ball there. ''The shore patrol had to work out there quite a lot to take care of the sailors who were unable to take care of themselves,'' says Lerner.

Once, Jim and Jan were boozing in Olongapo with a bunch of others. Curfew was approaching, but the crew was still psyched to party, so they blew off curfew and headed for some bars at White Rock Beach. Shore patrol found them, cuffed them and threw them in a paddy wagon. They spent less than an hour in the brig, and when they were released to their duty officer, he returned their IDs and told them to have a good time—once they were out of sight of the MPs. They were ordinary men doing an impossible job in an unwinnable war—a little wildness was tolerated, even condoned.

Jim knew how to party. It didn't matter how exhausted he might have been. On one deployment, according to Lerner, Jim and his merry band of pirates flew to Subic Bay in a four-engine prop plane on a trip that took nine days, making stops in Hawaii, Guam, and Midway. It was exhausting. Didn't matter. "Those guys went right to the barracks and right into town and Janos was leading the charge," he says.

Not that he wasn't a good troop. Always well-prepared, athletically skilled, and complying with every order, Jim "was dedicated and all the things you wanted to see," Lerner says. "In those days, there was a tendency to question orders. But you never got that out of him." Jim was never insubordinate, "he was just one of the guys stacking San Miguel beer bottles on the table."

Nelse recalls meeting up with Jim during his first year at Subic Bay. He hadn't seen him in five months. Jim told him he'd show him the town. They crossed the bridge and proceeded into the endless bars and smiling girls of Sin City.

"All these girls kept shouting at him," Nelse says. " 'Johnny! Johnny de Leon!' And they would make this hissing sound. 'SSsssss! Johnny! Johnny!' ''

Johnny de Leon was the Philippines' top celebrity at the time—a DJ of tremendous popularity; Nelse asked Jim what was up.

"Oh, I told them I was the DJ from Manila," he explained.

"It was one of those little things that he pulled," Nelse says. "Here we are, halfway around the world, and he seems like he's in his backyard."

But life wasn't all girls and San Miguel. Jim told Nelse that one night in Sin City he saw a pickpocket grab some jewelry from a bystander and tear off down the street. The local cop drew his weapon and the crowd—including Jim—fell on the ground. The cop shot the guy, dead square in the back.

"Jim never forgot that," Nelse says. "He was just incredulous."

Even if not in enemy territory, SEAL missions could be treacherous. They were frequently deep in the ocean, after all, a place that can be dangerous for all kinds of reasons.

One time, Jim and his platoon were scuba diving. They entered the forward hangar of a submarine, through which they were going to enter the body of the sub. The round hangar door, which was operated hydraulically, began to close while the men breathed through hoses allowing them boat air while in the hangar. But before the hangar door could close, a large shark appeared and began swimming right for them.

Their hearts started to race as the shark came closer and closer. Was it going to make it? Was it going to beat the door and actually end up locked inside the hangar with them?

The platoon lieutenant got on the underwater intercom. "Don't shut the door!" he yelled. "There's a shark coming in here with us!" But once the machinery was set in motion to close the hangar door, it couldn't be stopped.

Luckily, the shark turned and swam away at the last moment.

He did his job when called upon, no matter how dangerous—or distasteful.

"There were these two goofy little missions we went on in Subic bay," Lerner remembers. "We had to do a search for a dead body in the Olongapo River—which we called 'Shit River' 'cause it was basically an open sewer. The mayor [of Olongapo] had requested we find this guy—some Fillipino civilian who'd been drinking too much San Miguel beer. We swam in Shit River for hours. Eventually [one of the divers said,] 'Hey, I think I found him' and he held up this ankle.

"The other time, I got a call. We had a going away party for Larry Bailey. We were all pretty shit-faced but when we went back to the barracks we heard that these Filipino banditos were held up [in the water] under the supply area. So we raced down in swim gear . . . with our .38 pistols after partying all night and we finally caught these three guys."

It turned out that one of the three bandits was a local Filipino hood called "Boy Negro," who was wanted for seven counts of murder. It quickly became lore among the Filipino populace: " 'Don't fuck with UDT—they just captured Boy Negro.' From that point on," says Lerner, "we were revered as some bad dudes."

The SEALs' reputation among the Filipino populace continued to take on superhero status. As part of the Southeast Asia Treaty Organization, in 1971 the

SEALS simulated sneak attacks against British and Australian ships. When they finished their part of the exercise, however, many of the individual SEALs would climb on board and get drunk with the Brit and Aussie sailors. "I had to chase my men all over seven different ships," Lerner says. "My boys were going on board and drinking Fosters and getting shit-faced." Not long afterwards, the sneak attack mission showed up in a Filipino comic book, with the SEALs being the heroes of the wartime adventure.

As a civilian, and, especially, as a candidate for office, Jim Janos—as Jesse Ventura—has refused to talk in detail about his military career.

Critics have argued that his selective silence is unfair, since he brags about his military service for political ends. The license plate on his 1990 Porsche Carrera 4, for instance, reads UDTSEAL, and is framed in a holder that reads "Mess with the best/die like the rest."

During his campaign for governor, he was frequently seen on the campaign trail in a tight-fitting SEALs tee-shirt. And he is given to pronouncements like, "I've jumped out of an airplane thirty-four times. I've dove 212 feet under water. I've done a lot of things that defied death."[11] On the campaign trail, he constantly pointed out his status as a veteran, contrasting it with his opponents' cushy college days. He also continually cites his experience as a SEAL as all that's needed to prove he can be a governor.

And yet he refuses to say what, in fact, he did as a SEAL.

If it seems odd, it's not out of character. Using his military experience as a political tool while refusing to elaborate as to just what that experience entails, is just one of many examples of Jim's trying to have it both ways.

"Military is a personal thing," he has said. "It's however you choose to handle it when you're done, and it's no one's business but yours." This is enhanced by the story that he had no idea that his father had been awarded seven bronze battle stars during World War II until after his death in 1991, at age eighty-three.

He's also said that his reticence on his war record is due to a concern for national security. "I was ordered by my commanding officer not to discuss anything because of the nature of work the SEALs are," he said. "I was involved in one thing that I won't go into anymore, that could have been an international incident. Would you want me to come forward?"[12]

One of the rumors his opponents whisper is that Jim served in Vietnam, but "only" as a store clerk, so he didn't see any actual combat, and didn't actually perform any SEAL duties. This rumor is fueled by his Navy rank, "Storekeeper—third class."

But a rating of "storekeeper" doesn't necessarily mean that your job was as a supply petty officer, according to Bailey. Given Jim's youth, Bailey says, he probably wouldn't have assumed that duty. "There are 150 different ratings in the Navy," Bailey says. "They had those ratings because they had to have ratings." One Underwater Demolition Team might have fifteen officers, and 100 enlisted men, and maybe fifty different ratings. It was just a requirement. Just how things are done in the Navy.

Yes, Bailey says, certainly Jim was trained as a storekeeper and, as such, was instructed in how to issue "administrative-type things like boots, sleeping bags, knives, hammocks, and backpacks." But, according to Bailey, Jim "probably never worked as a storekeeper," he just "studied the storekeeper's manuals. An overblown analogy would be graduating from law school but never practicing law . . . We had mess officers on the SEALs teams but they very rarely ever cooked."

Despite suspicions caused by his reticence, members of Jim's platoon confirm that Jim *did* do serious and dangerous work, mainly hydrographic reconnaissance—maps of the underwater topography of the shorelines of both the Philippines and Vietnam.

According to a member of his platoon, Jim participated in a number of missions of inland reconnaissance into Vietnam itself. Once there, he and his platoon looked for anything that the enemy may have left behind. If they ran into the enemy, they assessed how many of them there were. But they didn't see a lot of actual enemy soldiers—more than 90% of their missions were at night. He wasn't stationed in-country, engaged in firefights like soldiers from the Army and Marines, but he was sure as hell doing his duty, occasionally even in enemy territory in Vietnam.

Paul Spark, a member of Jim's SEALs training class who was also a member of his UDT group in Subic Bay, argues that downing San Miguels—while a part of Vietnam life, as in every war—wasn't how they spent most of their time. "Part of the military life was social drinking—like on a college campus," Spark says. "We did have parties—you were living for the moment; there was a war going on. But we weren't a bunch of drunks." Jim took his job "very seriously," Spark says, "and was very professional. Everybody was."

THREE

THE DRIFTER

Active duty for Jim ended in December, 1973, but he remained in the Reserves until September, 1975. Like so many veterans before him, Jim had entered the military naive, childlike, very much a kid. When he left he'd been hardened, both physically and mentally. Jim now found himself, at twenty-two, with little direction for the future. The SEALs led him to believe that he could do anything. He almost chose a very treacherous path.

Between deployments, one of Jim's UDT teammates had gotten him interested in riding Harleys. Jim had gotten really into it, and while he was in the Reserves, his house off-base in Coronado "had motorcycle parts strewn throughout" it, according to Nelse, who lived with him at the time.

Membership in outlaw motorcycle gangs has swelled at two points in American history: immediately after World War II, and during and immediately after the Vietnam War. Before he'd been discharged, Jim began riding with a California motorcycle gang called the South Bay Mongols. The Mongols were a biker gang attempting to rise to Hell's Angels-like status. In the San Diego area at the time, the Mongols had two chapters, each with approximately thirty-five members—one in South Bay, and the other in El Cajon.

They put Jim through an initiation and before long he was wearing their colors on the back of his leather jacket. Back at the Naval Base, some of his superior officers were concerned.

After Jim was discharged, he rode with the Mongols for about six months. According to a former undercover investigator with the San Diego District Attorney's office, the Mongols "didn't have the criminal heart that the Hell's Angels had."

Jim hung with the crew and walked on the edge of their world. "They were a weird group," says Nelse. "I had never met bikers before, and they couldn't have been nicer." But, at least to Nelse, their dress and demeanor were bizarre. Led by their president—the aptly nicknamed James "The Fat Man" Rivera—the South Bay Mongols were social misfits, lovers of booze and hard living and the fringe. The women looked like they'd been around the block a couple hundred times—"like they'd been rode hard for awhile," according to Nelse.

"(We) partied, had fun, (and) rode Harleys," Jim has said. "It was a new adventure."

Many of the crew was clearly involved in criminal activities, but according to law enforcement investigators, it was mostly small-time stuff—bar fights, dealing marijuana and metamphetamines, maybe the occasional possession of a firearm.

Jim loved hanging with them, but he was wary of jeopardizing his future. When the cops pulled the Mongols over and searched them, Jim would be treated the same as the others, regardless of his military status. Once they saw his military ID, he told one reporter, the cops "tended to look at you and go 'What are you doing?' . . . They usually were pretty good to you, the police, because they realized you were military, so you couldn't be out breaking laws, because if you break a law in the military, you get double jeopardy. You get first tried by the civilian courts which are the easier ones, and when you're done with that you'll get tried by the military courts which are the tougher ones. So I didn't break the law when I was a biker.''[13]

So he tried to have it both ways, assuming a compromise that would enable him to have fun but also create a plausible deniability. Whenever they were about to engage in illicit activity, Jim's Mongol friends would ask him to go watch the bikes.

"I think it was just the novelty at the time," Nelse says of Jim's involvement with the Mongols. "It was something new to try. . . . He'd been in the military and had been conventional in his thinking and behavior for four years, so maybe he just wanted to stretch his wings and try something different. . . . But he could see right away that a long-term relationship with these people would not be in his best interest."

Jim's friendship with the South Bay Mongols is not as anomalous as it may initially appear. Sociologists have long recorded not only the strong libertarian streak present in outlaw motorcycle clubs, but other trends that meshed perfectly with Jim's personality. One noted sociological study observed that 1970s-era motorcycle gang members were not necessarily "violent, but are impulsive"; that members "are not especially hostile towards most social institutions such as family, government, and education"; that most members had finished high school, and many were veterans. Like Jim, bikers love to shock more conventional members of society.

Perhaps most consistent to Jim's evolving political

philosophy was the importance a biker gang placed on
autonomy, "the form of freedom . . . central to the outlaw biker expressed philosophy," according to one so-
ciologist's study, which manifested itself in a "studied
insistence that they be left alone by harassing law enforcement agencies and over regulating bureaucrats . . ."[14]

"People have the wrong idea of what the bikers
are," Jim has said. "The bikers are just people that
believe in living that lifestyle. It doesn't necessarily
mean that you're some criminal, you know. You just
like a free experience of riding Harleys . . ."[15] And
since BUD/S training, Jim now had a danger jones, a
need to live on the edge—riding motorcycles helped
to quench that.

"At that point in time, in a motorcycle club, you'd
always end up in jail," Jim has said. "But they were
nice guys. There's bad in everything."[16]

According to the San Diego District Attorney investigator, Jim's claims of full membership in the
group is probably more myth than reality. "A lot of
people were wannabes," he says. "They might have
put on a jacket"—with the Mongols trademark black-
and-white colors—"but they weren't out there com-
mitting the crimes that some of these other people
were."

"We pretty much kept kind of a running tally on
these people, who belonged and who didn't," he says.
And Jim Janos's name never came up. "We couldn't
have kept track as far as all of the associates or
hangers-on," the former investigator says. "They
might have a rally where 400 to 500 people show up,
but maybe only forty to fifty were actual members."

If Jim was actually a member, then "he should have
a big old tattoo on his shoulder that says 'Mongols

Motorcycle Club,' '' the investigator says. ''You
didn't get to become a member without a tattoo. . . .
A lot of people liked the camaraderie and the drinking
and the dancing and the rock and rock and all that
kind of crap.'' But many of these people were not
members.

If Jim would later exaggerate his role with the
South Bay Mongols, claiming full-fledged membership when he was probably just a prospective member,
it's just as well. By 1977, a war had broken out between the Hell's Angels and the Mongols, leaving
many Mongols gunned-down or dynamited. By 1982,
even The Fatman was cooperating with the DA,
snitching on five other Mongols accused of killing an
Angel.

Luckily, by then Jim had left the Mongols behind
him. In early 1974, he'd moved back to Minnesota.

He was adrift, rudderless, with a sea of choices before
him and no idea of what to do or where to go. In the
spring of 1974, Jim had enrolled at North Hennepin
Community College, a two-year school in Brooklyn
Park, Minnesota. That summer, perhaps still thinking
about someday playing for the NFL, he went out for,
and won a place on, the North Hennepin Community
College football team.

Number 70 clearly stood out from the other players.
With his muscular bulk, long hair and Navy *chutzpah*,
Jim didn't quite fit in with the other players, many of
whom were just kids. But he liked being different and
getting attention—after a tackle, Jim would tear off
his helmet and wave to the crowds as he ran back to
the huddle.

His career on the North Hennepin team didn't last
very long. Very quickly, Jim had begun butting heads

with the team's coach. As a Vietnam War veteran, it was tough to take the coach very seriously; it was tough to take the game seriously, either. He quit before long.

"I soured on football real fast," he said in an interview. "I was a twenty-two-year-old freshman, and after four years in the Navy, I'd played man's ultimate game, which is war. There is no way I could view football the way the coaches did—as a life-and-death struggle."[17]

Like a lot of students at North Hennepin—where the mean age for a student is twenty-six—Jim, an average student in high school, seemed a bit insecure about his intellect. The man who had survived Navy SEALs training, the Vietnam War, and the South Bay Mongols was afraid of freshman English. But at college, according to one of his teachers, Professor Tom Bloom, Jim discovered the capacity for learning within himself. Like a lot of North Hennepin students with low expectations, Jim was stunned to discover his abilities.

Bloom was impressed, too. "His verbal facility was very great," he says.

Bloom taught the thirteen students in Jim's class a combination of writing and literature with real-world applications. They read short stories—D. H. Lawrence's "The Rocking Horse Winner," James Joyce's "Araby," Bernard Malamud's "Magic Barrel." On their midterm exam, Jim got the highest grade in the class. Though his grades were almost all A's (except for one B), Bloom remembers Jim mainly for his contributions to class discussions. "He's a good talker," Bloom says. "He's very funny, very endearing."

He tried his hand at other activities as well. The director of a college play wandered into the weight room one day to recruit a Herculean character. The pumped-up Jim was "discovered" and appeared in the play early in March, 1975. (In an interesting preface to Jim's future gubernatorial campaign, the play was Aristophanes' comedy *The Birds*, about two Athenians who seek to escape from their city because it's choking with corrupt politicians.) He took a theater class, even thought about majoring in drama.

He also worked as a bouncer at a biker bar called the Rusty Nail Tavern, located in suburban Crystal. He'd gone in looking for a job and had been turned down, but a few nights later, he wandered back in and the owner approached him. He asked Jim if he was the Navy guy who'd just been discharged and had been in the bar looking for work. Jim said yes. "Hire him," the owner said.

The bar hosted a lingerie show every day at noon. Jim liked working there.

One night, Jim found himself up in the front of the stands at the Minnesota Armory watching a pro wrestling bout. It starred "Superstar" Billy Graham—a "Bad Guy" who strutted his stuff, bowed and preened for the crowd, holding the audience in rapt—and enraged—attention.

Graham was huge, with a pumped-up body out of Greek mythology by way of Venice Beach. He had bleached-blond hair, and 22½-inch biceps, which he would constantly flex.

"When I saw him and saw how he had total control of this crowd," Jim would later recall, "I said, 'That's what I wanna do.' "[18]

Pro wrestling had enjoyed varying degrees and trends of popularity throughout the country. At the beginning of the twentieth century, pro wrestler Frank

Gotch was a hero who enjoyed Babe Ruth-like status. A bout between Gotch and another wrestler held in Chicago's Comiskey Park in 1911 drew a crowd of 28,000—at that time the most highly attended athletic event in the country, excluding horse racing. Gotch was twice invited to President Teddy Roosevelt's White House, and there was even talk of him running for governor of Iowa before he dropped dead in 1917.

Having drawn packed houses to Madison Square Garden during the Depression, the sport increased in popularity after the advent of television. "It was hot on TV in the late forties and fifties since it was so easy to shoot," says Mike Chapman, executive director of the International Wrestling Institute and Museum and author of six books on the subject. But it soon dissipated in widespread acceptance, and retreated to a localized system of promotion. "Wrestling has always gone through cycles," Chapman says.

It was still huge in Minnesota, however, where the American Wrestling Association (AWA) was almighty, enjoying a following not unlike what an NBA team experiences today. The AWA was run by Verne Gagne, from Excelsior, a wrestling phenomenon since the 1940s who was a University of Minnesota All-American and an alternate member of the 1948 Olympic team. Gagne had made a very successful jump to pro wrestling, and had been based in Minneapolis since the sixties, where the AWA offered bulky guys who could wrestle and stir up the crowds a shot at a living and a modicum of fame.

"At the time, it was one of the biggest territories in the world," recalls Eddie Sharkey, who wrestled professionally from 1961 until 1971 and began training pro wrestlers soon afterwards. The AWA's territory "stretched from Chicago to Winnipeg, and from

Green Bay to Omaha—and everything in between. . . .
To wrestle here was really big stuff. . . . We got more
wrestlers here in Minneapolis than any other city in
the United States. I don't know why; there's something about Minnesota, I don't know, we still can't
figure it out.''

"In high school we'd have clubs that would orga-
nize trips to see pro wrestling matches," says Brett
Anderson, who grew up in the seventies and eighties
in St. Paul as the son of Wendell Anderson, the governor of Minnesota from 1970 until 1976. "It was definitely something that I didn't miss watching.''

These were the things Jim knew about himself: He
enjoyed the spotlight. He had an impish sense of humor that endeared him to others. He was clever, if
uneducated. He loved to be the center of attention, and
he loved to do so in a provocative way. He also knew
that, though he was a good athlete and an impressive
physical specimen, he wasn't going to make it as a
pro football player.

"The war was over . . . life goes on . . . Probably
wrestling was a great outlet for him to release some
of these pent-up frustrations and anxieties," pro wrestling's "Gorilla" Monsoon, a colleague of Jim's, once
speculated.

Was this a world he could enter? He wandered into
the Seventh Street Gym, co-owned by Sharkey. Maybe
there was a place for Jim in this business. Maybe this
was a real career possibility. He certainly had no other
ideas.

The Seventh Street Gym, at Seventh and Hennepin
Streets in downtown Minneapolis, was, according to
Sharkey, "one of those great old gyms—a real shit-
house." There Jim could see not only pro wrestlers,
but four or five boxers being trained by Sharkey, and

his partner Ron Petersen. When he was in town, even "Smokin' " Joe Frazier would stop by.

Jim approached Sharkey and told him he wanted to turn pro. Could Sharkey help him? Sharkey agreed.

"The thing I liked about him the most was his great sense of humor," Sharkey says. "And he's the most honest man I ever met in my life. The old Seventh Street Gym had every crook in the world; he stood out there as an honest guy."

Jim worked hard, training almost every day, determined and focused. "He was a very good student," Sharkey recalls. "He was smarter than the rest—he was also going to drama class to learn how to be a good speaker." Since Jim was already in such great shape—engaging in fifteen hours of weight training a week, and downing twelve raw eggs and thirty different vitamin pills a day—Sharkey didn't need to train him how to lift weights or work on his endurance. So Sharkey began with the basics of wrestling—how to fall, how to protect himself, take-downs, and actual moves.

"Finally, we had an actual match," Sharkey remembers. Since the deputy mayor was friends with Sharkey, he came down to watch, as did the Mayor of Minneapolis at the time.

Jim won the bout. But only because Sharkey accidentally hit the ref.

In September, 1974, on a Thursday night at the Rusty Nail—Ladies Night—Jim, working the door in a sports jacket and turtleneck, saw one of the most beautiful women he'd ever seen. Thin and sexy, with long brown hair with blonde highlights, she had arched, impish eyebrows, a button nose, and a wholesome smile that shot arrows into his heart. Their eyes met.

She was Teresa Masters, she said. She'd just turned nineteen. She'd graduated from St. Louis Park High School, and was living with her uncle in Minnetonka while she did secretarial work in the area.

Terry was the daughter of German Lutherans who lived in Vernon Center, a rural area outside Mankato, Minnesota, an hour or so south of Minneapolis. Jim was smitten immediately. Terry was funny, extroverted, flirty, and of good Midwestern stock. She had attended charm school at thirteen, and had started riding horses when she was just a toddler.

Even though she was only nineteen, Terry had grown completely confident and comfortable around men. She also happened to know a great deal about pro wrestling—Jim was amazed that she'd even heard of "The Crusher," much less that she remembered when he was a Bad Guy.

He asked her out. She said yes.

Jim had told her that they were going to the Yacht Club, so Terry bought new clothes. But the snooty-sounding "Yacht Club" turned out to be a dive bar called the Schooner on the south side of Minneapolis— a cheesy low-rent joint where brawls were common and one of the main selling points was that you could spit tobacco juice right onto the floor. While they were there, cops came in to arrest a man who'd been beating the crap out of his girlfriend.

"Who are these people?" Terry thought.

But forgetting the stink of the Schooner or Jim's macho exterior, Terry saw something in Jim that was soft, even sweet. While he projected a large boldness to the world, when it was just Jim and Terry it was just Jim and Terry and he was quiet and gallant.

That was it. They were both sold. They started an intense relationship.

Soon enough, Jim even brought Terry by the gym and introduced her to the guys. It must have been true love, the guys thought.

FOUR

JESSE "THE BODY" VENTURA

Wrestling is to pro wrestling as policy is to politics. Pro wrestling is a sport that relies on larger-than-life personae and complicated storylines that justify grudges and feuds. Crowds come not just to cheer for their heroes, but to jeer and boo the villains. Often, in fact, the Bad Guys, or heels, are bigger draws than the Good Guys or babyfaces.

The white-trash kabuki follows the same basic script: Before the fights, both Bad Guys and Good Guys are paraded before the fans where they're interviewed. As one former pro wrestler wrote in a dime-store guide to the sport in 1976, "The heels radiate hate and evil . . . the babyfaces project an all-American boy image. The heels rant and rave and shout like insane animals as they insist that they will demolish their opponents. The babyfaces insist they'd rather stick to the rules but, if the bad guys get out of line, they (the good guys) will employ killer tactics to destroy them."[19]

Jim, a controversial, troublemaking character ever since his teenage years, wanted to be like his wrestling idol, "Superstar" Billy Graham—a heel, a Bad Guy. But the name "Jim Janos" wasn't gonna cut in the world of pro wrestling. This was a sport filled with names like "Flying" Antonino Rocca and "Gorgeous'' George. His name would need to do more than just describe his new pro wrestling personality, it needed to arouse knee-jerk hatred in all who heard it.

He looked at a map of California. He'd decided that his pro wrestling character would be a Bad Guy, a California surfer dude with more than a touch of the style of the megalomaniacal Graham. Everyone hated California surfer dudes—especially in arctic Minnesota.

"I bleached my hair blond, because people dislike blond men, especially if they know their hair's been dyed," Jesse remembered in an interview. "I wore my hair down to my shoulders and tried my best to look like a surf bum who did nothing but work out on the beach and chase women all day."[20]

The blond look worked immediately. Even before he'd begun wrestling professionally, Jim would go to local matches and other fans would heckle and pick fights with him because of his blond mane.

Let's see, he needed a name that would conjure forth everything evil about that ilk . . .

His eye settled on a small city on the beach, north of Los Angeles. Ventura. Yeah, Ventura. He'd always liked the name Jesse, and ''Jesse Ventura'' meshed well . . . Yeah, that was it.

He had his new name. From now on he would be ''Jesse Ventura, the Surfer.''

The year 1975 was a big one for Jesse Ventura, the Surfer. On July 18, he and Terry married. It wasn't the most extravagant wedding in Minneapolis history; the couple gathered with an intimate crowd in Timothy Evangelical Lutheran Church, a small church in St. Louis Park, outside the Twin Cities. The band only knew a few songs—''Proud Mary'' and three polkas. The band members' amazingly obvious toupees kept sliding off their heads. And as if that wasn't enough, the photographer they'd hired had a heart attack during the event. But for Jesse and Terry, it didn't matter.

Almost immediately after his wedding, Jesse hopped a charter flight to Johnstone, Pennsylvania, where he was scheduled for a wrestling meet. Because 1975 was also the year that Jesse's career as a pro wrestler began.

Sharkey made a few calls for him. Jesse wasn't good enough for the AWA; he needed to spend some time in the minors. In April 1975, Sharkey told Jesse to report to Bob Geigel, who ran the National Wrestling Alliance circuit, a wrestling organization that featured small bouts throughout Missouri and Kansas. Jesse got in his beat-up Chevy and drove off to Kansas City to begin his pro wrestling career.

He had $250 in his pocket. But he was immense—fifty-two-inch chest, thirty-four-inch waist, nineteen-inch biceps. Sometimes he was even mistaken for his idol, "Superstar" Billy Graham.

Jesse followed Geigel's direction pretty well: In his first match, at an arena in Wichita, Kansas, he threw his Good Guy opponent—Omar Atlas—over the ropes and was disqualified. It was what he'd been told to do.

It was small-time stuff—the wrestlers earned $35 to $65 a match, maybe getting a couple hundred dollars a week and driving all over the state. It was always a random sum, what Jesse called a "chef's surprise." In his first six months, he never was paid more than two figures at a time.

"It was where a lot of young wrestlers who were inexperienced went," says David Meltzer, writer of one of the premier insider pro wrestling publications, *Wrestling Observer Newsletter*. "Or veterans with nowhere else to go." In his first year as a wrestler, Jesse made very little money. He stayed in a fleabag hotel that cost $23.50 a week.

Regardless of the grim surroundings, Jesse had hope. Geigel saw something in him, he said.

"Kid," Geigel said, "stick it out in this business and someday you're going to make a lot of money."

"He was in Kansas City for a couple months when he called and asked what he should do," Sharkey recalls. "I suggested he go to Oregon since there was more money there at the time." Sharkey told Jesse to call Don Owen, who ran the pro wrestling organization out there.

So Jesse moved on to Oregon, where he wrestled as a Bad Guy in Portland, Eugene, and Salem. He traveled all over—putting 128,000 miles on a car in less than two years—and worked exhaustively, once wrestling every night for sixty-three consecutive days.

After a meet, Jesse would shower and line up to see whoever was promoting the fight that night—in Portland, it was Don Owen, in the small southern Oregon towns, it was Elton. When it was your turn to see Elton, he'd give you your bills while he'd cough out—in a cranky old voice—something like, "Well, we didn't draw that good tonight, guys." Every now and then he'd slip the wrestlers an extra $5 for beer money, tell 'em not to tell nobody that he did so. He said the same thing to everybody.

Saturday night bouts in Portland were televised, and scored huge ratings. Jesse—a fairly poor wrestler— nonetheless prospered there "because he was a good interview subject," according to Meltzer.

"I will do what I have to do get people down to watch me," Jesse Ventura, the Surfer, told the North Hennepin Community College newspaper in 1975. "If it means saying something to rile the fans, I'll do it. The more people I rile, the more who will pay to see me lose, so the more I'll make myself.''

As it had in high school and as a Navy SEAL, his strong-looking physique—augmented significantly by his wit and bluster—enabled him to grow popular, to ''get over,'' as they say in pro wrestling parlance. ''He was well below average as a wrestler,'' says Meltzer, recalling one particularly uninspired bout Jesse had with Moondog Mayne, a skilled wrestler. ''That match was pretty bad,'' Meltzer says. Still, Jesse ''was one of the better personalities.'' Taking a page from ''Superstar'' Billy Graham's book, Jesse would do his homework on each city, researching the local sports teams and any issue he could use to antagonize the crowd.

On the road, Jesse would try to avoid temptation whenever possible. While his fellow wrestlers would go out drinking after an event, Jesse would keep away from barroom troubles, locking himself in his hotel room, calling Terry every night, and maintaining the discipline he'd learned in SEAL training.

''He stayed in his hotel room,'' Sharkey says. And when he was wrestling in Minneapolis, instead of having a beer with the fellas, ''he'd just go straight home. He wanted to be with Terry. A lot of guys in the wrestling business, they go down the toilet, and get involved in drugs and drinking, but he never did.''

During the day, Jesse would watch soap operas; his favorite was *The Young and the Restless*. As with wrestling, he found soaps compelling—full of stark good versus evil battles and all sorts of nefarious characters. In *Y&R*'s ''Victor Newman,'' a character who joined the soap in 1980, Jesse would find a kindred spirit to his new persona—an irresistible villain.

Most pro wrestlers at the time would work the

Oregon circuit for two years. While there, Jesse fiddled around with his persona: Calling himself "The Great Ventura," he wore a mask—"to hide his good looks." Unmasking him became a gimmick. In 1978, an announcer noted Jesse's physique and started called him "The Body." It stuck.

Another pro wrestling gimmick spelled the end of Jesse's time in Oregon. He'd been in the state for so long that—as was standard—he had switched from Bad Guy to Good Guy status. The promoter set up a big match between Jesse and Buddy Rose, an area villain who'd been in Oregon forever. The "feud" between them was hyped. The match would be "Loser Leave Town." Jesse lost and moved back to Minnesota.

Of course, as with all pro wrestling, the outcome of the meet was pre-determined. By the spring of 1978, Jesse was now deemed ready for Gagne's AWA, one of the largest leagues of the two-dozen or so in the country at the time. So Jesse lost and moved on to his next gig, back home in Minnesota.

In Jesse, Gagne—a former Olympian—saw a great actor but a crappy wrestler. He encouraged Jesse to talk trash. He would have to. Even after a few years, "as a wrestler, he was pretty bad," says Meltzer. "By today's standards, he'd be considered horrendous."

One AWA colleague remembers an early eighties meet Jesse had against Maurice "Mad Dog" Vachon in Winnipeg, Manitoba. "Jesse went over to Mad Dog to do a 'collar-and-elbow hookup,'" the friend recalls, "and he steps on his shoestring and falls flat on face. I thought, 'My God, what kind of a match is this gonna be?' Then Mad Dog took the microphone [from announcer "Mean" Gene Okerlund] and hit him over the head and beat the shit out of him."

"He'd just come in from Portland and Kansas City, working scrub territories to polish his act," recalls legendary announcer "Mean" Gene Okerlund, who worked with Jesse in three different leagues, including the AWA, and to whom Jesse bestowed his everlasting nickname. "It wasn't universally accepted that he was a 'wrestler'.... He was not a great worker in the ring. But he was such a communicator that he could always play the part of a Bad Guy and always get people riled up."

"As a performer, I'd give him a seven or eight; as a wrestler, give him a one," Gagne once said. So Gagne "put him in a tag team where the other guy could wrestle but couldn't talk. Jesse could talk but he couldn't wrestle."[21]

The other guy was Adrian "Golden Boy" Adonis. Adonis grew up in Buffalo, was an abysmal student, got in gang fights and ended up playing semi-pro football in Canada. After learning the ropes of wrestling in Texas—he offered $5,000 to anyone who could pin him in less than ten minutes—Adonis originally met Jesse in Portland, though they didn't team up until their AWA days. The team became one of the AWA's biggest draws.

Jesse, returning to his Bad Guy status, knew his role in the duo was to rile the crowd. He devoted his energies toward "getting people mad enough at me to pay to come see me get my ass kicked. I did whatever it took to put their keisters in the seats." He had a family to support, now, after all—son Tyrel was born in 1979.

It was tough on Terry. Jesse was on the road a lot—too much. Sometimes he had fifteen fights in a month. It wasn't unheard of for him to travel thousands of miles in just a week. But life was easier for Jesse in the AWA than it had been it the smaller leagues. Gagne didn't promote seven-day-a-week events, and after they'd wrestled in the twelve-to-sixteen matches Gagne set up each month, wrestlers could take some time off.

Terry was still central to Jesse's life, and, despite his Bad Guy image, in reality he continued to walk on the straight-and-narrow. "He pretty much stayed to himself," Okerlund says. "On the road a lot of guys get their nose in trouble, especially with broads, booze, and pills. Jesse stayed clear of that. After the gate, he'd grab something to eat and go to bed."

Jesse's mom was proud of her son's job, even if she was a little deluded about its genuineness. "She thought it was wonderful," recalls Bill Ritter, "but you didn't dare tell her it wasn't real. It was real to her. If you wanted to have a fight with Bernice you just start telling her it was all fake."

In the ring was different, though. Jesse's character had evolved into a truly vainglorious and loathsome individual. He constantly posed, flexing his immense biceps, straining his pecs into well-defined orbs, showing off his wide Jersey-bull back for all to see. He would stop fighting mid-bout and start flexing, or brushing back his long hair.

Under pressure from promoters, Jesse had bulked up to epic proportions mainly by taking anabolic steroids. From 1978 until 1982, Jesse had steroids injected twice a week for five weeks or so, then refrain for half a year or more. He's said that he quit taking steroids as soon as he learned the damage they can wreak on the human body. "I don't think even he denies that he was on the sauce," Okerlund says. "He was cut like you wouldn't believe."

His costume was equally flamboyant—brightly colored tights, wacky sunglasses, bulky dangling earrings, a feather boa, and a bandanna or hat to cover his rapidly balding pate. He grew what hair he had long, and dyed it blond, or purple, or green. His face sported a beard or sideburns or mutton chops or a Fu Manchu.

"I'd pose in the ring and tell the crowd, 'Take a look at this body, all you women out there, and then take a look at that fat guy sitting next to you who's eating pretzels and drinking beer,'" Jesse recalled in an interview. "'Who would you *really* rather be with?'"[22]

"I'm the most beautiful man in wrestling today, without a doubt," he said in a ringside interview, as the fans booed him. "I'm from CaliFORNya," he said in his thick Minnesota nasal twang, "In CaliFORNya, everybody poses . . . People pose at the supermarkets, they pose in the used-car lots, they pose everywhere. I'm the master poser. In CaliFORNya, it's Jesse THE BODY! IT'S JESSE THE BODY EVERYWHERE!"

"I liked him because he was terribly creative," Okerlund says. "He took pride in keeping his gimmick fresh. He was very big on current events" and made a lot of pop culture references. It was simple to interview Jesse, Okerlund says, because he actually had a brain. "What he would do in a three-to-five minute interview was great. And easy. I'd just ask him a few questions and he'd roll, and it was a conversation after that."

A 260-pound mass of bluster and ego, Jesse was a hit. His favorite moment from his time with the AWA was in 1980, when Jesse was one of the main attractions selling out the St. Paul Civic Center for the first time—one of the highlights of his life. There were thousands of rabid fans, all screaming, in unison:

"Jes-SEE SUCKS! Jes-SEE SUCKS! Jes-SEE SUCKS!"

The razzing went on for five minutes while Jesse sneered and flexed and posed. Then, he told the crowd to kiss his ass.

It was "very thrilling," he later said. "I literally had that crowd in the palm of my hand."[23]

He became a huge feature in the AWA, and a local celebrity. In 1981, he even got to introduce the Rolling Stones at the St. Paul Civic Center. He was on a roll.

The late seventies were also a time of Jesse's first political awakening. In Minneapolis, he became interested in the Stop the Draft movement. As he explained to C-SPAN in December 1998, his experiences in Vietnam led him to conclude that the draft was unfair and discriminatory.

"When I grew up, if you had money and lived in the suburbs, you got to go to college, and didn't have to worry about going to war," he said. "But if you were growing up from working class and you had to get a job out of high school, well then you got sent to war. . . . The draft was the most unfair piece of garbage that this country ever put together."

His time in Vietnam has also made him, politically, someone who would only use military force in the most extreme conditions. "The only way to justify a war, in my opinion, is that [the President] has to say 'Would I go?' or 'Would I send my son?' And if he can say that he would send his son, then it's justified."

He wasn't sure that the U.S. involvement in Vietnam had been justified, and he felt for the soldiers who'd been left behind. After noticing an MIA bracelet on a bank teller, Jesse began wearing MIA bracelets, each one honoring a Vietnam soldier whose whereabouts are unknown—a practice he continues today. "They answered the call of our country and our country has failed to answer their call," he has said.

During those few years, Jesse also supported his first political candidate—DFL Senate candidate Joan Anderson Growe. And he took Terry to an Equal Rights Amendment rally at the state capital.

"If you don't go, then don't gripe," he told her.

"At one time, I thought he was the most liberal guy I'd ever met in my life," says Okerlund. "He was always very topical, and could always discuss the issues of the day, even back in '78." He talked a lot about environmental issues, Okerlund says. "He always said that they were screwing up the lakes."

The New York-based Capitol Wrestling Corporation was run by Vince McMahon, Sr., who had carved the northeast as its piece of the pie. After Jesse did a TV taping for Vince Sr.—for which he was paid $50— Vince Sr. asked Jesse to come on board his organization for six months, from January to June, 1981, to wrestle his heavyweight champion in major city after major city. Jesse jumped at the chance, and Gagne put out the word that Jesse had been "suspended" for his outrageous behavior.

As Jesse drove east, he was psyched for the opportunity to work with Vince Sr., who was not only the biggest promoter in the country at that point, but also one of the nicest and most considerate. Jesse thought Gagne was an asshole—he yelled, he screamed, he wasn't at all Jesse's kind of guy. Conversely, he could walk into Vince Sr.'s office all pissed off and walk out feeling good; the old man just exuded goodwill.

Jesse lived in Connecticut during that time. Sometimes, during his drives back to Connecticut from eastern Pennsylvania, he would have anywhere from $6,000 to $10,000 in his pocket. He enjoyed the opportunity to work with the bigger organization. Vince Sr. even flew Jesse to Tokyo once, to wrestle Antonio Inoki. (Interestingly, Inoki was later elected to the Japanese Senate.)

After six months in Vince Sr.'s big league, however, Jesse returned to Minnesota and the temper tantrums of Verne Gagne. Jesse wanted to take the summer off, so he'd asked Vince Sr. to keep it quiet that he was heading back to Minnesota. He didn't want Gagne to bring him back immediately. Gagne found out anyway, however, and announced on TV that Jesse's suspension had been lifted. Jesse went back to the AWA. Sick of depending on the "chef's surprise" in paychecks and the capricious whims of the owners and fate, Jesse also ran a gym. It was a safety net, a way for him to exert a modicum of independence.

The two dozen or so separate geographical fiefdoms in pro wrestling had, for generations, enjoyed a gentleman's agreement, maintaining friendly relationships in which cooperation was the norm. In the early 1980s, however, with the growing markets of cable TV and pay-per-view, there was too much money pouring into the sport for that diplomacy to survive.

McMahon's son, Vince Jr., didn't think his old man had been running the operation right. Having joined the operation in 1968, Vince Jr. thought the business about each wrestling company staying in its own territory was just plain stupid.

Vince Jr. was a handsome, muscular man, with the bouffant of a fifties lounge singer and the ego to match. "They never understood the kind of man I am," Vince Jr. once sang, on an album featuring wrestling stars. "I do my own thinking, got a lot of big plans. I'm a man running wild, heading for the top. Never slowing down, never going to stop. Along the way, you're going to see a lot of men drop.''

In 1982 Vince Jr. bought out his father, changed the name of the organization to World Wrestling Federation (WWF), and threw away the gentleman's agreements of the past. The sport was never the same.

''McMahon is totally responsible for the leagues not cooperating anymore,'' says Meltzer. ''But if there was no Vince McMahon, inevitably it would have happened anyway with someone else.''

Vince Jr.'s first stop was a TV station quite outside of the WWF's territory—3,000 miles away, actually, in southern California—that had expressed interest in running the WWF's programming. Then Vince Jr. hit a St. Louis station that was willing to air WWF's bouts as well. It was previously unheard of to broadcast wrestling meets from other territories, and Vince Jr. rapidly made enemies.

Vince Jr.'s next stop was the talent pool of the AWA. With offers of more cash and fringe benefits, and big plans to expand not only across the country but around the world, Vince Jr. had little problem stealing away AWA headliner Hulk Hogan in 1983. Vince Jr. soon began taking away talent from all over—and receiving death threats from rival promoters as a result. The old guard was furious.

In the early summer of 1984, Vince Jr. phoned up Jesse.

''Jesse, I want you to come work for me,'' Vince Jr. said. He told Jesse what the plan was, how successful they were all going to be. Jesse had made $100,000 in 1982 with the AWA, but Vince Jr. spoke of even more money than that. ''Do you want to be a part of it?'' he asked.[24]

By then, Jesse detested Gagne. Terry had given birth to their daughter, Jade, the year before in a delivery fraught with complications and grave medical ramifications. She had a rare form of epilepsy and terrifying seizures; doctors weren't sure she would survive. Then, at the age of nine months a routine DPT (diphtheria, pertussis, and tetanus) shot caused her permanent neurological damage. Jesse thought that Gagne had been totally insensitive to his plight. "The man had no compassion when I, you know, with my daughter's situation," Jesse would later say in a legal deposition.

Jesse would do it. But he'd need to give Gagne thirty days notice.

"What for?" Vince Jr. asked. "You're never going to work for him again. You're going to work for me from now on. It doesn't matter."

Jesse told him that he'd have to talk it over with Terry. He'd get back to him soon.

That night, Jesse and Terry went out to talk about the risk he'd be taking by hitching his wagon to Vince Jr.'s stallion. It was risky, and he'd be burning his bridges with Gagne, no question. Maybe even burning his bridges with every member of the old guard, because they hated Vince Jr. and what he was doing. There was a chance that, if Vince Jr.'s plan failed, Jesse might never wrestle again.

Nonetheless, they decided to go for it.

Jesse called Vince Jr. and accepted the offer—though Vince Jr. would have to verbally guarantee him that he could work for the WWF for the next seven years. Vince Jr. agreed to this, according to Jesse.

"Well," he said to Vince Jr. as he was getting off the phone, "I guess I better go have the showdown with Verne now, walk in and tell Verne I'm leaving for the WWF."

"Why do that?" Vince Jr. asked. "Send him a tele-

gram. Because it's only going to cause trouble, Jesse.
You're going to go in there and Mr. Gagne is going
to get mad. You're going to get mad. There could be
a fight, even physically. You don't need that. We don't
need that."

So Jesse sent Gagne the telegram.

The gamble paid off. Thanks to Vince Jr.'s ruth-
lessness and business acumen, WWF shed pro wrestling's cult status and the "entertainment sport"
became accepted by mainstream America. WWF wrestling was fast becoming a trend among yuppies, a
place for eighties-era celebrity synergy with Mr. T
(who wrestled); Cyndi Lauper (who "managed" a
woman wrestler); and Cathy Lee Crosby, Elvira and
Susan St. James (who did ringside announcing in
WrestleMania 2).

Jesse reaped the rewards of Vince Jr.'s acumen. In
1984, Jesse and Adrian Adonis were the subjects of a
profile in *People* magazine. In 1985, Jesse—dubbed
"wrestling's Goldilocks"—was featured alongside
Los Angeles Lakers coach Pat Riley and baseball superstar George Brett in *Sports Illustrated*'s moments
of the year. CBS sold hundreds of thousands of albums
featuring the musical stylings of fifty wrestlers—Jesse
among them. Jesse even had his own single, called
"The Body Rules."

On March 31, 1985, WWF began hosting
WrestleMania, the first of its unprecedentedly enor-
mous pro wrestling events, selling out Madison Square
Garden. By 1987, the WWF was grossing $145 mil-
lion. Jesse even bought a Porsche Carrera with his
share of the royalties from his WWF action figure.

And the sport grew, it changed. "Jesse was one of
the first guys in WWF who was like a comic book
figure, who combined flashy dress with a huge

pumped-up body,'' says former pro wrestling fan
Daryl Kessler, a childhood fan of the WWF in the
seventies and eighties. "There were always big strong
guys, and there were also guys who were more flashy,
but Ventura definitely seemed to usher in an era that's
probably still around today, the era when everything
became over-the-top. And after he came around, I
started to lose interest because it was a lot more yelling and screaming and pumped-up superheroes as opposed to wrestlers.''

"The way that pro wrestling changed (as the WWF
grew), mirrored the way that pornography changed,''
says Chris Haber, a pro wrestling fan from Buffalo,
NY, who saw Jesse wrestle alongside "Nature Boy"
Ric Flair when he was growing up. "In the seventies,
it was less mainstream, and the women in pornography
looked like real women. Then it got big, and you had
the pumped-up bodies and this surreal showmanship.
It was very Reagan-era. Same with pro wrestling.''

Some pro wrestling fans thought that the sport lost
something when it got so huge. Former fan Kessler
remembers seeing a Ventura-Adonis tag-team at Long
Island's Nassau Coliseum that ended his interest in the
sport for good. "I literally saw a match that followed
the same script that I had seen on TV from Madison
Square Garden that month,'' Kessler recalls. "And
even though I always thought wrestling was fake, it
was that match that, like Jesse himself, took it over
the top, and made me realize that it was just a ridiculous sport to follow.'' That was the flip side of the
increased presence of television in the sport—fans
could see, for the first time, that the sport was, indeed,
choreographed.

Jesse and Adrian—called The East-West Connection—saw their tag-team events hyped larger, and

their salaries increased to up to $10,000 a match (plus a cut at the gate). Their antihero histrionics continued. "We're the rule breakers," Jesse said. "It's something a wrestler finds out early, an inner ability to piss people off,"[25] He continued trying to piss people off whenever possible. "We need the fans, but that doesn't mean I gotta like 'em," he said. "I've grown a great dislike for 'em."

In the *People* profile of The East-West Connection, Jesse is described as working with a Twin Cities anti-draft group, and having "a glib, growling, and broadly informed political consciousness. ('[President Reagan's Secretary of Defense] Al Haig scares me; he's like Darth Vader,' [Jesse] says. 'They should put him on grass for a year.')"

Terry accompanied her husband on one trip to New York City's Madison Square Garden. She was amazed at the rabid lunatics—mostly hecklers booing Jesse—crowding around the rear entrance of the arena. After the limo managed to make its way into the garage, the attendants lowered the garage door, though it remained open a crack.

"It was quite a scene," Terry recalled. "They were down there on the ground, in the mud, with their faces all scrunched up, and they were yelling at us." Jesse went over, and talked to them, charming the beasts. "If they get to talking to him, they like him," Terry said. "If he can get their attention, he can sway anybody."[26]

"I rode with he and his wife from the Helmsley Palace to Madison Square Garden in a limo," Okerlund says. "He was just the toast of the town. They loved him."

Fans of pro wrestling had good reason to hate his character: He was truly evil. "Win if you can! Lose if you must! But always cheat!'' Jesse would cry. He would be rude to announcers—including Vince Jr.— as well as his Good Guy opponents.

"The Body!'' he would say to the crowds, firing them up. "The most brutal man in wrestling! The sickest man in wrestling! Mr. Money! Mr. Charisma! Mr. Show Business!''

Some wrestling insiders say that Jesse's out-of-control ego wasn't entirely an act. From the moment "Classy'' Fred Blassie, Jesse's WWF manager, met Jesse, he didn't like him at all. "He thinks he knows more than anyone else,'' Blassie says. "I wouldn't say he's smart . . . I didn't care too much for him. He wouldn't listen. He did what he wanted to do.''

One time during the taping of a WWF event in Pennsylvania, "Gorilla'' Monsoon gave Jesse specific instructions. But Jesse's ego was rapidly expanding, and he seldom obeyed orders. "He was told to stay in the corner, he and his team partner, Adrian Adonis, because the camera was set right for the corner,'' Blassie recalls. "But talking to him was like talking to the wall. He did what he wanted to do. He started walking around.''

After the match, Monsoon approached Blassie. "I thought I told you that Vince said to keep him in the corner.''

" 'I told him that,' '' Blassie responded. " 'What are you going to do—want me to hog-tie him?!' ''

Jesse was unquestionably a popular figure, but he was just one of many, and his schtick was more as a windbag than anything else. His specialty was in pre- and post-game interviews, not so much inside the ring.

"He just wouldn't listen,'' Blassie says. "He'd be in the ring too long. He wouldn't tag Adrian Adonis so Adrian could get in there.''

Jesse's one signature move was "The Black-breaker," in which he'd grab an opponent around the waist and hoist him across his shoulder. Then Jesse would hop up and down, shaking the man—supposedly breaking his lumbar vertebrae—until he gave in. It was a move that required a lot of strength, but not much skill. Jesse, after all, was known as having a limited repertoire in ring, and not being very agile.

He loved to be nasty—sometimes it seemed like he drew strength from the crowd's hatred. He brought his "always cheat" philosophy to new lows. During a 1984 arm-wrestling match against Ivan Putski in St. Louis, Jesse—supposedly enraged—grabbed Putski, threw him on the table, and began smashing him with a metal folding chair. It was a fairly typical affair: Jesse's character was proud of being a cheater.

Other wrestlers were much more popular. "I didn't pay too much attention to him, because he wasn't one of my top men," Blassie says.

Hulk Hogan was huge, clearly WWF's pre-eminent star. Elbowing out Jesse for a place in the limelight were "Rowdy" Roddy Piper, "Macho Man" Randy Savage, Big John Studd, and the Junk Yard Dog, among others.

That would soon change, as fate intervened—in a near-fatal incident—and allowed Jesse to carve a special niche for himself that he might otherwise have never stumbled into.

FIVE

JESSE "THE BODY" VENTURA–COMING TO YOU RINGSIDE

Throughout 1984, Jesse toured thirty cities throughout the country with his arch-rival Hulk Hogan, hyping their upcoming World Title bout in Los Angeles.

He would call Terry from the road, uncharacteristically complaining. He hurt, he would say. He was in pain. He was fatigued and short of breath. Terry was worried. Though the "competitions" and outcomes of pro wrestling bouts were, of course, fake, the sport nonetheless did demand a lot of the wrestlers physically. Though the punches may have been pulled, wrestlers did injure themselves quite often.

In San Diego right before the Hogan fight, Jesse was stricken with a pulmonary embolus. A blood clot that started in his leg broke lose from its vein and proceeded through his body to one of his lungs, where it hindered the effectiveness of his breathing. Not enough oxygen was getting in to his circulating blood, and not enough carbon dioxide was getting out—too much of which can be poisonous. If treated ineffectively, a pulmonary embolus can be fatal.

Jesse was rushed to the hospital. Doctors performed an angiogram and rushed him into intensive care.

Terry was relaxing at their home in Brooklyn Park, Minnesota, when she got a phone call from a "Dr. Amstein." *Who?* she thought.

"You have to get on the next plane and get to San Diego at once," the doctor commanded her.

"Why?" she asked.

"I don't want to get into it over the phone," he said.

Terry grabbed the next flight and sat with her husband while he lay in critical condition for six days. The hulking mass of bravado had never looked even remotely vulnerable to her before, and now here he was, at death's door, helpless in a hospital bed and only thirty-three.

She was afraid he wouldn't survive. Every night she'd go back to her hotel room, call her mom back in Minnesota, and bawl her eyes out.

Luckily, the doctors were able to get Jesse out of trouble. He returned to Minnesota and was a convalescent for almost two months.

"See?" Bernice told her skeptical colleagues at the hospital. "I told you pro wrestling was real."

The entire experience was the lowest moment of his life—not least of which because he was out more than a million dollars because he had to cancel the fight. And though Jesse recovered, his wrestling career—the only real job he'd ever had—had been sidelined for good.

He had to think about his family, their future. Ty was five and Jade was one. Jesse was thirty-three and had been wrestling for nine years. What could he do?

Through his participation in local celebrity golf tournaments, Jesse had met Tom Ryther, the sports director of KARE-TV, the Twin Cities' NBC affiliate. In the late fall of '84, Jesse phoned Ryther up and asked to meet with him.

"Tom, I don't know if I'll ever be able to get back

to the ring again," he said. "I would like to have a shot at being a sports broadcaster."

Making such a proposal took some serious cojones. Jesse had no experience in announcing or sportscasting, and he knew even less about being a reporter. Most sportscasters spend years out in the boondocks honing their craft and learning as much as they can before trying to crack a Top Twenty market like the Twin Cities. But Jesse—with his interesting combination of ego and desperation—was proposing that he be given a shot anyway.

Ryther hooked Jesse up with another guy at the station who gave Jesse a cameraman and a producer and told him to give it a shot. He wasn't going to be paid—he was just going to be given the opportunity. It was more than most other wannabe reporters got.

Pop star Cyndi Lauper had been a marginal figure in pro wrestling, casting "Captain" Lou Albano in her videos and going on to manage WWF women's champion Wendi Richter. Lauper was in town, so Jesse called her manager, David Wolf, and explained his predicament.

Would he let her interview Lauper? Wolf agreed.

Jesse went over to interview Lauper, who had multi-colored hair, and, on camera, she dyed Jesse's hair four different colors. Jesse was amusing, and the producer and cameraman worked hard at combining the footage with information about Lauper's involvement in pro wrestling.

The station loved it, splitting it into two parts and running it during sweeps. Jesse didn't even have time to work anything out with KARE-TV's station managers before Vince Jr. got wind of Jesse's project and gave him a call. He wanted Jesse to do color commentary for the WWF—but as a Bad Guy, as a heel.

"We had this talent who had this tremendous gift of gab and great charisma," Vince Jr. told NBC's *Today Show*. "What do you do with him when he can no longer wrestle? So he became a commentator."

As a wrestler, Jesse was fair-to-middlin', but as a commentator he was at the top of his craft.

"Right out of the gate, he was very good," Okerlund says. "If someone else was talking, Jesse was listening and thinking. He developed a very quick wit."

WWF bouts appeared in syndication throughout the country, and the first pay-per-view *WrestleMania* event was broadcast in 1985, with guest referee Muhammad Ali. Also that year, NBC began showing *Saturday Night Main Events* as an occasional alternative to *Saturday Night Live*. Its ratings, in fact, often surpassed the comedy show, once scoring the No. 1 ratings event for that time slot.

And Jesse "The Body" Ventura was up front and center for many of these events. Though it can be argued that being one of the wittiest announcers in pro wrestling isn't entirely unlike being one of the best-looking members of a leper colony, Jesse nonetheless saw his distinct portion of the celebrity universe only increase in scope.

He would return inside the ring for a few matches in '85 and '86, but they were mid-card bouts, few and far between. His appearances were most of a curiosity than anything else—"Hey look, the TV announcer is wrestling." No one took him seriously as a wrestler anymore. Some fans whispered that Jesse had been sidelined as a result of being exposed to Agent Orange during the Vietnam War.

Jesse was happy to return to the ring, though. "I'm

the first announcer in history that is going to step into the ring and back up what I say," Jesse said to another announcer. "Do you think you'll ever see [former CBS sportscaster] Brett Mussberger put on a pair of cleats and go nose-to-nose, and toes-to-toes with [former Chicago Bear William] 'Refrigerator' Perry?"

"He became so popular that every company that did wrestling had to put a Bad Guy in there to do color," Meltzer says. "Some were bad, some were better than him, but he was the one who made the mold." His booming, gravel-voiced braggadocio—a Bad Guy dissing the talent in the ring, rooting for the other Bad Guys, and hyping himself with wit and mean-spirited snipes—became an industry standard.

At first, he was nervous. During his first *WrestleMania* telecast, Jesse's co-announcer Monsoon once recalled, Jesse was shaking like a leaf. Monsoon had to hold Jesse up by the back of his pink tuxedo jacket.

The character of Jesse "The Body" Ventura would take center stage whenever he could, ignoring the other wrestlers except to insult them or root for the other Bad Guys—"Ravishing" Rick Rude, The Honkytonk Man, Andre the Giant. He preached a very eighties ethos: "When there's money involved, there ain't no friends!" he proclaimed during the twenty-man Battle Royale of *WrestleMania* 2 in 1986. "The pleasure is all yours," became his signature line.

Much of it was new, some of it was funny. He called Ricky "The Dragon" Steamboat "a wimp"; he said the Ultimate Warrior had "a million-dollar body and a ten-cent brain"; he flirted with Elvira and Vanna White. He constantly mocked Gorilla Monsoon—("Gah-RIL-lah," in Minnesotan)—for being old and immense, Hulk Hogan for being vain and balding, and occasional co-announcer Vince Jr. for being over-bearing. "I'm here to call it like it is!" he said. The fans ate it up. During *WrestleMania* IV, Jesse was called out of the broadcasting booth to pose to the cheers of tens of thousands.

"Jesse was Jesse twenty-four hours a day," Monsoon once said. "It wasn't something he turned on when the cameras were turned on. It was genuine. It was who he was."

Jesse started out salaried at $1,000 a week, but eventually, he and Vince Jr. worked out a deal where he was a free agent, an independent contractor with no health insurance or other benefits, paid by the event. Work increased so much, Jesse later recounted that "it was hard to determine what month of your life you were in."[27]

At the beginning, Jesse was paid around $800 for the first few *Saturday Night Main Events* for which he did color commentary. But by 1987, he was raking in $7,500 for each *Main Event*, $5,000 for each *WWF Superstars of Wrestling* taping session, $10,000 for taping *The Survivor Series* in '87, $15,000 for three days' work for the *Slammy Awards*, $20,000 for *WrestleMania IV*, and $12,000 for the 1988 *Summer Slam*. Jesse's agent, Barry Bloom, made sure that Jesse's payment increased each year.

Though Jesse was paid good money to deride Good Guys like Hulk Hogan, the bad blood between them was real.

"Verne Gagne and Hulk Hogan are probably the only two people Jesse hates," says Ed Sharkey. Their feud is known as a "shoot" in the world of pro wrestling, Okerlund says—meaning that they actually, really, truly dislike one another.

"That was all Jesse," says an executive at World Championship Wrestling. "Jesse would insult Hulk, he would start things. It was never Hulk."

Some speculate that Jesse was always jealous of Hogan, and it's not tough to see why. They both came from the AWA, were blond and pumped-up. But Hogan became the sport's biggest star, while Jesse was a mid-card player who spent most of his career on the sidelines, off-camera, talking about other wrestlers.

And Hogan eclipsed Jesse despite the fact that neither man was exceptionally talented in the ring. "Hulk Hogan is not a great wrestler, either," Okerlund says. "I'd put Hogan in the class of Ventura. He's gotta a couple of bumps he can do . . . and that's it."

"Jesse's been pretty mean to Hogan," Okerlund says. "He always called him a knockoff, saying he knocked off every Jesse move—when meanwhile, Jesse knocked off every one of his moves from 'Superstar' Billy Graham."

There may have been more substantive reasons for Jesse's animus as well. Supposedly Jesse had once floated the idea of organizing WWF performers into a union—and Hogan, who had acted all buddy-buddy with his fellow performers, had tipped off Vince Jr., who squashed the effort. Jesse never liked or trusted Hogan after that.

Occasionally Jesse's commentary could be seen as misogynist or racist. Jesse's rather ignorant attempts at humor weren't anomalous—pro wrestling has long been derided as one of the last bastions of ethnic and cultural stereotypes. Indeed, its characters frequently depend upon them—a Native American was bequeathed with the moniker "Chief Strongbow," a notorious Japanese manager named "Mr. Fuji" would bow to his opponents, and crowds booed the Soviet-

Iranian tag-team duo Nikolai Volkoff and The Iron Sheik in the name of patriotism.

Sometimes it crossed the line. To psyche out his African-American opponent in 1990's *WrestleMania VI*, "Rowdy" Roddy Piper painted the right half of his body black, dancing Michael Jackson-style and criticizing his opponent's "bug eyes" and "dilated nostrils" in his pregame interview.

Jesse occasionally fed this ignorance as well. During the first *WrestleMania*, Jesse described the psyche-out moves of the Junk Yard Dog, another African-American wrestler, as "a lot of shuckin' and jivin'." During *WrestleMania III*, Jesse said that the middle name of Koko B. Ware, another African-American wrestler, was "Buckwheat."

"Gimme a break, Jess," Monsoon said.

"Oh yeah!" Jesse said. "He told me he has a brother, too. Named Stymie. Wears a derby!"

Jesse then started referring to Koko B. Ware as "Buckwheat."

"Vince made him stop saying the Buckwheat stuff," Meltzer reports. "Jesse was bitter about it. He complained to me, 'I asked Koko and he said he thought it was OK.' "

"It was something we really shied away from in those days, any comments racially motivated or discriminatory," Okerlund says.

Jesse walked the same line with Latinos, purposely botching Tito Santana's name—calling him "Chico" Santana.

"I betcha Chico wishes he was back selling tacos in Tijuana right now!" Jesse said as Santana got pummeled during *WrestleMania IV*'s tag-team championship.

"He's not from Tijuana, Jesse," Monsoon replied.

"Doncha love Chico's music, Gah-RIL-lah?" Jesse said to Monsoon in 1990's *WrestleMania VI*, as Santana came to the stage to the background accompaniment of Latin American music.

"That's *Tito*," Monsoon corrected. *"Tito."*

"It reminds me of a blue note club in Tijuana . . ." Jesse went on, "I used to go there when I was in the Navy a lot."

"I think you must have picked up something there, Jes," Monsoon said.

"Oh, I picked up something there, Gah-RIL-lah," Jesse responded. "More than once. Let's see, there was Juanita . . ."

"Let's not go into it," Monsoon said. "Just forget about it."

Another time, when manager Bobby "The Brain" Heenan appeared at *WrestleMania IV* in an unusual outfit, Jesse said, "Heenan looks like a Chinaman, don't he?"

Jesse, playing the role of Bad Guy announcer with verve and gusto, also tiptoed down the line of misogyny. In the late eighties, one pro wrestling storyline pitted "Macho Man" Randy Savage against his former partner, Hulk Hogan. As described in a sociological study of pro wrestling published by the University Press of Mississippi,[28] Savage's "manager," Miss Elizabeth, symbolized a "disruptive force and was marked as a catalyst for the degeneration of the idealized manly bond between" Hogan and Savage. "Face commentators Mean Gene Okerlund and Gorilla Monsoon sympathetically, albeit ineffectually, insisted on her position as victim, imagining her inner turmoil, while the heel commentator Jesse Ventura railed against Miss Elizabeth's meddling in particular and women in the ring in general. Gorilla repeated attempts to deflect Jesse's misogynist rants."

"What a golddigger she is," Jesse sneered.

"Why does [Savage] keep bad-mouthing Elizabeth, Jes?" Monsoon asked. "Why don't he leave her alone?"

"She deserves it!" Jesse responded. "She oughta be in his corner, doing what she—Hey! He took her to the top, Gah-RIL-lah."

"He also slapped her all around in the dressing room, didn't he?" Monsoon pointed out.

"Who the hell was Elizabeth before she got with 'Macho'?!" said Jesse.

Later Monsoon and Jesse argued over a Savage ploy. "If there's something there you can use to your advantage, why not?!" Jesse asked.

"If it means knocking a woman down or taking her out of the picture, 'Do it'?!" Monsoon asked.

"With what Elizabeth has pulled, hey, a punch in the nose might not be so bad for her," Jesse said.

"Please," said Monsoon.

"Wrestling's a very sexist sport," says *Wrestling Observer Newsletter*'s Meltzer.

Certainly, on its most basic level, judging a pro wrestler's sensitivities to women and minorities is just plain silly. Pro wrestling, after all, is hardly a venue for enlightened—or even remotely educated—entertainment. After all, how much political correctness can you expect in a sport that features midget pro wrestlers named "The Haiti Kid," "Little Tokyo," "Lord Littlebrook," and "Little Beaver"?

Nonetheless, Jesse appeared more than willing to embrace themes and give voice to dialogue that certainly can be seen as ignorant—offensive, even. And he was decidedly not joined in such jeers by Monsoon. Pro wrestling is no less valid a venue of popular culture than television or movies or literature or music or the Internet. And—especially when you consider how popular pro wrestling is among adolescent males—it is no less important for pro wrestling to refrain from embracing ugly attitudes than it is for, say, rap music or Hollywood blockbusters. While Jesse's role as a Bad Guy necessitated obnoxiousness, it is unclear that it needed an injection of prejudice.

After years of listening to Jesse's schtick, a few fans found Jesse's act growing a bit stale. Some complained that he thought he was the star of the show, not the actual wrestlers. He wasn't. Jesse's name doesn't appear on any of the name-packed *WrestleMania* videocassette boxes, though even managers like Bobby "The Brain" Heenan and Lou Albano, ring announcers like Yankee manager Billy Martin, and special guests like Run-D. M. C. and Morton Downey, Jr. merited inclusion on the bill. Announcers just aren't the draw, and Jesse's name didn't really mean that much to fans.

Not that you'd think that based on Jesse's rhetoric. "You just remember something, Gah-RIL-lah," Jesse proclaimed to co-announcer Monsoon during *WrestleMania VI* in 1990. "Sean Connery was voted the sexiest man of the year with my hairstyle! I have Paul Newman's eyes, Kirk Douglas' chin, and Robert Duvall's haircut!"

Regardless of the anti-Jesse murmurs, many fans still loved him, agreeing with the *Toronto Star* reporter who called Jesse "the best color commentator in the [wrestling] business."

Soon Jesse's opinions on other areas of sports, too, would be in demand.

In 1989, the Tampa Bay Buccaneers were in a world of trouble. Their abysmal performance on the field was being matched by equivalently weak fan attendance. The Bucs were having a tough time getting even 14,000 fans into the seats for home games.

Challenging times call for drastic measures. Bucs management approached popular local rock station Q105 about broadcasting its games. "They were trying to change the image of the team," says Randy Kabrich, then the program director for Q105. "They were a horrible team."

After a year of broadcasting the hapless Bucs, Kabrich realized that nothing much had changed on the field. "They still had not done a lot to improve the team," he says. "So if there wasn't going to be a show put on by the Bucs, I decided that we were going to have to put on a show on the radio. . . . We would have to blow out all the old-line ways of thinking and doing football."

Kabrich was splitting his time between his Florida gig and LA, where he served as operations manager for KQLZ Pirate Radio. Both stations were enjoying much success with the wacky "Morning Zoo" format—jokes and schtick and attitude and multiple voices.

Kabrich was still working on his Buccaneers problem in June 1989 when, out in LA, a buddy of his called him up.

"Let's go out to see some pro wrestling," he suggested.

"You're nuts," Kabrich said. "I have no interest in that stuff."

But his friend was going with Jesse Ventura, a former pro wrestler, and an announcer for the WWF, as well as with Jesse's agent, Barry Bloom.

"C'mon," he said. "It'll be fun."

"So after some arm-twisting and not having any-

thing better to do, we went out to the matches,'' Kabrich recalls.

As they walked into the area, the fans noticed Jesse
and—even though a match was going on—they
started chanting for him instead of the match.

''Jes-SEE! Jes-SEE! Jes-SEE!''

Jesse looked embarrassed by it, Kabrich says, and
later apologized to the wrestlers for inadvertently up-
staging them in the middle of their match.

''But I saw the reaction he got there,'' Kabrich
says. He started thinking.

After the matches, Kabrich and Jesse were driving
around when Jesse started talked about how he wanted
to get into other forms of broadcasting other than
WWF.

''I gotta find someone to do color for me for the
Bucs,'' Kabrich said.

''I'll do it!'' Jesse replied.

When he was working for NBC Sports in the seventies, Kabrich had seen former pro athletes announce
sports other than their own. So after a few conversa-
tions, he wasn't worried about Jesse's ability to broadcast. He was even less worried about Jesse's ability to
bring some spice to the table.

For play-by-play, Kabrich hired Gene Deckerhoff,
the voice of Florida State University football. ''I didn't
feel that Jesse alone would be right doing color,'' Kabrich says. ''I felt he needed someone to play off of.''
Kabrich also picked Al Keck, the sports director for
Tampa's CBS TV station, a man who lived in Tampa
and knew the Bucs up, down, and sideways.

Bucs management had to approve all of Kabrich's
choices, however, and it hated the idea of bringing
Jesse to the broadcasting booth. Hated it. ''They were
adamantly against Jesse from early on,'' Kabrich says.

"They claimed we were, quote, 'trying to make a mockery of the team,' unquote."

Kabrich countered with the observation that it was tough to make the Bucs any more of a mockery than they already were with their pitiful record. But the Bucs' GM and coach were against signing Jesse.

Kabrich called Jesse and told him to hang tight. "I knew I was going to get it through," he says. "It was going to take some political maneuvering." First step was getting them to allow Jesse to do the pre-season broadcasts.

"Believe me, we'll get them," Kabrich told Jesse. "We just need to let them see how good it will be."

By the time of Q105's press conference in fall 1989—the night before the first pre-season game—rumors had shot through town that the former pro wrestler might be part of the equation. "We were in Tampa stadium," Deckerhoff recalls. "Keck and I were in the locker room, and the media was waiting. Then in walks Jesse and everybody roars—'cause the rumor had been rampant."

Jubilation aside, the big question for the reporters, of course, was just what in the hell did Jesse know about football? "Look, I was in the service and I played football in the service," Jesse said, according to Deckerhoff. "I played in high school, and I've followed football—in particular NFC Central football since I'm a Vikings fan. I know the Buccaneers."

Three men in the booth? And one of them a former pro wrestler? Everyone was curious to see if it would work.

"Essentially what happened at seven o'clock that night was the predecessor to Fox Sports—it was sports with an attitude," Kabrich gushes.

"I laid out the X's and O's," Deckerhoff says, "Al

knew the players, and then Jesse would come from the left wall, right wall, forward wall of the ceiling and say, 'I like the way that guy's hittin'—that's real football.' I think from day one we had that thing going better than Kabrich had ever thought.''

After the game ended, the team's owner even came into the broadcast booth and insisted on shaking everybody's hand—including Jesse's.

"That's the most amazing broadcast I ever heard," the owner told the team.

"Then he asked me if we could get Jesse for the whole season," Kabrich recalls.

Jesse brought his endearing bluster to the Tampa Bay job, though it was significantly downplayed from his pro wrestling persona. When the Bucs faced off against the Bears at Soldier Field in Chicago that November, Jesse showed off not only his macho persona, but also a spiteful thin-skinness as well. A sports columnist for the *Chicago Sun-Times* had written a column harshly dissing the Bucs.

"The gist was, 'Load up on this one, because the Bears are going to kill the Bucs,' " Deckerhoff recalls. The *Sun-Times* reporter ''called the Bucs 'the milquetoast pastel pantywaists of the Trocs.' So, in the pregame Jesse just unloaded on the columnist. 'Who is this guy calling us the 'pastel pantywaists'?!' Throughout the broadcast, he was making allusions to it.'' After the Bucs won a last-second field goal, Jesse commented, 'Not a bad performance by the 'milquetoast pastel pantywaists of the Trocs,' right, Al?''

On one level Jesse's commentary during that second Bears game is typical root-root-root-for-the-hometeam bravado. But on another it can be seen as part of a personality pattern visible throughout Jesse's public life—especially after he became involved in politics: Jesse constantly displays a hypersensitivity to criticism from the media. He often reacts disproportionately, giving his adversaries more of a platform than they deserve.

Kabrich and Deckerhoff say that generally, Jesse was a hit and a consummate professional. Opponents' broadcast teams would ask to interview Jesse for their half-time show. He was a huge attraction for fans in every stadium.

The three-man team lasted two seasons. After the 1990–1991 season, a different radio station bought the rights to broadcast Bucs games and made an effort to not sound like Q105 had—the new station decided it wanted to return to the nuts and bolts of the sport. Deckerhoff and Keck stayed, but they canned Jesse, bringing in a former Bucs nose tackle who knew much more about both the sport in general and the team in particular.

Jesse's questionable commitment to the Bucs indubitably contributed to his firing as well. In his second season, he missed at least a month's worth of broadcasts because he was in Toronto working on a film. Then, directly as a result of his work on the movie—which required that he stand in a flimsy costume in water in northern Canada in the middle of the winter—he got sick and missed a few more broadcasts. His heart was clearly not with the Buccaneers, and it showed.

"Mean Gene," he told Deckerhoff, "in this movie I got a love interest."

It was all part of Jesse's latest plan: to become a movie star.

SIX

CO-STARRING JESSE VENTURA

The larger-than-life go-go eighties brought forth a slew of high-testosterone, lowbrow cinematic fare. Schwarzenegger and Stallone ruled the silver screen, and movies featuring explosions the size of Rhode Island were the norm. It was a lucrative business: As movies dumbed-down, bloodied-up, and replaced dialogue with special effects, they became easier to market overseas. Demand for product—*any* product—increased significantly as cable, pay-per-view, and local video rental stores popped up in every city, town, and county throughout the nation.

In this atmosphere, pro wrestlers found Hollywood more open-minded about casting opportunities for their ilk. The behemoths had more showmanship than other athletes—like, say, football players—and were eager for the work, cash, and whatever continued adulation they could get. The seven-foot-four Andre the Giant shone as the sweet-natured Fezzick in *The Princess Bride*; Tiger Chung Lee appeared alongside Eddie Murphy in *The Golden Child*; and Hulk Hogan starred in his own crapabration, *No Holds Barred*.

In 1986, when Jesse responded to the casting call for the Schwarzenegger vehicle *Predator*, his professional acting experience had been almost entirely inside the ring. Whatever he lacked in off-Broadway thespianism, however, he more than made up for in physique—and all the casting call had asked for was a six-foot-four, 250-pound killer. It didn't sound like much of a stretch.

Barry Bloom, Jesse's agent, read the casting call and immediately phoned up casting director Jackie Burch.

"You gotta meet this guy," Bloom said. Jesse was paid $800 to appear on an episode of TV's *Hunter* in 1985, and Bloom had confidence that there was more work out there for Jesse if they hustled.

Burch says that she was in particular looking for Vietnam vets. "That was a very important thing to me," she says. When she heard about Jesse's status as a Navy SEAL, she was impressed.

Jesse walked into the Hollywood office. His hair was bleach-blond and shoulder-length. He was wearing a half-dozen earrings and his trademark Fu Manchu mustache. He was menacing in appearance, but a sweetness lay behind his husky voice. He looked all man, but seemed like a little boy.

She had Jesse read a couple lines. He wasn't perfect, but could take direction well. And as for his persona, he was a natural, she thought. A real character.

"Let's go meet the producer," she said.

Burch brought him to see Joel Silver. Silver agreed with her instincts; the part was his.

Such a quick casting decision made perfect sense to Lou Pitt, who represented Schwarzenegger as an agent with ICM, and augmented Bloom's efforts by serving as Jesse's agent around that time as well. "It's obvious that Jesse's presence is extraordinary," Pitt says. "He walks in a room and there's no place that he can hide, and he enjoys it. Some people can use [such a presence] effectively, and Jesse was certainly one who could use it effectively.'' For those efforts, the producers of *Predator* would pay him $5,000 a week.

Filming took place in Jalisco, Palenque, and Puerto Vallarta, Mexico in 1986. Jesse flew down on April 8, 1986, the day after finishing up his broadcasting at Los Angeles Sports Arena for *WrestleMania 2*.

The director, John McTiernan, Jr., was, like Jesse, thirty-five years old. He had only directed one other feature film—1986's *Nomads*—though he would go on to become an influential force in the action/adventure genre as director of *Die Hard*, which was released in 1988.

The actors were big and brawny. In addition to Schwarzenegger and Jesse, the cast included Carl Weathers—Apollo Creed from *Rocky*—and a host of character actors whose muscles and faces may be familiar to the average moviegoer, if not their actual names. Jesse and Schwarzenegger hit it off immediately. Jesse admired Schwarzenegger for any number of reasons. In particular, the money-conscious pro wrestler respected Schwarzenegger's self-made success. ''Schwarzenegger came into this country in 1970 with nothing,'' Jesse once said. ''and today people say he's worth $60 million. To achieve all that in less than twenty years tells me that Arnold is one very smart cookie.''

Jesse also could relate to the movie star's ability to constantly set new goals for himself, to be perpetually changing and adapting, a whirling dervish of self-improvement. ''Arnold looks in the mirror and sees his limitations—and also knows that his limitations will be as different in two years as they were two years ago,''[29] Jesse said.

And apparently the feeling was mutual. ''Schwarzenegger really liked him,'' Schwarzenegger's former agent, Pitt, recalls. "They were certainly cut from the same cloth. They were outdoors guys, athletes, they like to play practical jokes. They really enjoyed each other's company."

Pitt remembers Jesse as having a political bent even in the throes of filming a sci-fi action flick in the jungles of Puerto Vallarta. "Events and politics were very much a part of his life early on and he clearly was socially and politically motivated," Pitt says. "He was always conscious of issues. And he told me he wanted to get into politics," Pitt recalls, with a clear tone of bemusement in his voice.

"I said, 'Good luck.' "

Predator is 107 entertaining minutes of hackneyed bravado, big guns that go boom, and a high-tech alien critter.

Its plot is fairly simple: A commando team is sent to a nameless South American country to locate a cabinet minister and his aide whose chopper went down on the wrong side of a hot border. Once they get closer to the guerrilla camp in which the minister and his aide are imprisoned, however, it becomes clear that there's more to the mission than Schwarzenegger and his six-man team have been told. An alien monster with chameleon-like camouflage skills keeps capturing American soldiers—including a battalion of Green Berets—and skinning them alive. As the creature starts to pick off Schwarzenegger's men, the mission becomes: Kill the Alien.

The cigar-chomping Schwarzenegger plays Dutch, leader and—by the end—sole survivor of a team that includes a Native American with extraordinary tracking skills, a tough African-American who shaves with a knife, two white guys who are difficult to distinguish from one another, and Jesse. (The then-unknown Jean-Claude Van Damme was originally cast as the predator, but Van Damme was decidedly not a tough Vietnam vet, and reportedly he kept whining about how hot it was in the suit. He was soon replaced, though being cast in the film was how he first got his Screen Actors Guild card.)

Jesse—with long wisps of hair clinging to his balding head—plays Blain, a machine-gun totin', tobacco-chewing macho man in an Australian bushman's hat. He is the *mas macho* of the team; his first line comes when his fellow commandos decline his chewing tobacco:

"Buncha slack-jawed faggots around here," he says. "This stuff will make you a goddamn sexual Tyrannosaurus, just like me." Soon afterwards, he spits tobacco juice onto Weathers' shoes.

Much has been made of Jesse's most famous line from the movie: "I ain't got time to bleed." But the line is actually an example of the ridiculousness of Blain's over-the-top bravado—his fellow commando responds somewhat condescendingly, saying "Uuuuh, okay. You got time to duck?" right before an explosion that nearly kills them both.

According to Jesse, he had to fight for every line. "They were giving a lot of my lines to someone else," he recalled to Hollywood's *Daily Variety*. Jesse wanted to discuss this problem with producer Joel Silver, but he was told time and time again that Silver was "in a meeting" and couldn't see him.

"Finally I kicked open the door and said, 'We gotta talk,' " Jesse said.

"They gave me back my lines."[30]

He was right to fight for them; Jesse only had eight or so lines in the film. Blain is the second member of the commando team to be killed by the alien; the character dies before the movie is half over, though his corpse is dragged along for seven or so minutes after being gutted. Still, Jesse's performance in the picture is strong and perfectly suited to the genre; he distinguished himself as someone with a possible future in films.

Jesse has said that the premiere of *Predator*—which was released on June 12, 1987—stands as one of the professional highlights of his life.

"That was a trip into the Twilight Zone," he said of his first night on the press junket hyping the movie. "From south Minneapolis to riding on a private jet that holds like 14 people, and there are only two or three people on it beside the pilots, and to be staying in hotels where the cheapest room was $800 a night. I left to do that press junket with $234 in my pocket and my credit cards, and I returned never having used my credit cards once and with $234 still in my wallet."[31]

He liked being waited upon. In Chicago for the press junket, he asked one of the various lackeys for some chewing tobacco. The assistant returned with a shopping bag full, asking, "Is that enough?"

"I thought, 'God Almighty, I could service Major League Baseball with what you've got for me,'" Jesse has said.[32]

The film scored mediocre reviews. "*Predator* begins like *Rambo* and ends like *Alien*, and in today's Hollywood, that's creativity. Most movies are inspired by only one previous blockbuster," wrote Roger Ebert in the *Chicago Sun-Times*.

But movies like *Predator* are usually fairly critic-proof. It did well, earning about $60 million in box office and another $30 mil in rentals. It was even nominated for an Academy Award for best visual effects.

Jesse's fans from his wrestling days were impressed with his abilities. "Back then it was such a big deal when a wrestler did something other than wrestling," says *Wrestling Observer Newsletter*'s Meltzer. "Jesse did real movies with real actors. . . . Hulk Hogan did stuff out of wrestling, but he was always Hulk Hogan the wrestler." Jesse, however, seemed like he might have a second career at hand.

(Later, fueled by his gubernatorial win, Jesse gushed that he was "known for *Predator* even more than Arnold Schwarzenegger . . . As much as it's [Schwarzenegger's] film, I think I stole it.")

Jesse was excited about it, and thrilled about his new buddy, Schwarzenegger. Things that Ah-nuld said he would remember and take as gospel.

"[Schwarzenegger] said, 'Jesse, never read the script until the money's right," Jesse relayed once. "And I said, 'Arnold, that's very easy for you to say. You've got a dozen of them on your desk every day.' You know? And he said, 'No, the reason is this. First, if you read the script you might be biased and accept less money to do the role because you like the script. Second, if you read the script and never do get the money right, then you've wasted your time.' And he goes, 'Jesse, we have no time to waste.' "[33]

There were other reasons for his interest in both Schwarzenegger and his career. "I found out what kind of money Arnold makes," Jesse once said. "I wanted to get into that."[34]

Schwarzenegger enjoyed Jesse's company so much, he made sure the ex-wrestler was cast in his next project, *The Running Man*, directed by Paul Michael Glaser—"Starsky" of *Starsky and Hutch* fame.

"They did get along very well," says Burch, who

also cast *The Running Man*. "And again, *The Running Man* called for all these huge guys and Jesse was good for the role" of Captain Freedom, a retired jock and sports announcer. "He had done all that announcing."

Based on a short story written by Stephen King under another name, *The Running Man* is set in the American police state of 2017, where a "sadistic game show" is the most popular TV program of all time. Hosted by Damon Killian—aptly portrayed by Richard Dawson of *Family Feud* fame—"The Running Man" gameshow pits prisoners against a cast of "Stalkers," pro wrestling types who are armed and dangerous.

Schwarzenegger plays Ben Richards, a former policeman imprisoned for a crime he didn't commit and forced to be a contestant. In the course of his victories, Richards ends up not only falling in love with Amber Mendez, played by Maria Conchita Alonzo, but killing Killian and revealing to the world how corrupt both the gameshow and the government are.

Jesse again satirized himself in the film, though the role was even closer to reality than the overblown soldier of *Predator*. As "Captain Freedom," Jesse plays an egomaniacal former Stalker who now does color commentary for the show. Wearing a wig of thick brown hair, and the network's blue blazer over a white turtleneck, Captain Freedom is the essence of over-the-hill former-jock lameness. He hosts an embarrassing morning workout TV program in which he spews forth "No pain, no gain" clichés, stares admiringly at a poster of himself in his prime, and is interrupted by Killian when his color commentary becomes tiresome. It was pretty close to home.

After Richards has wasted the show's four Stalkers, Captain Freedom is ordered to come out of retirement and kill him. He refuses, delivering a soliloquy about the impurity of the current "Running Man" show, that could easily have been delivered by Jesse during his color commentary for WWF.

"I don't need this garbage," Captain Freedom tells Killian, storming into the control booth in the midst of putting on his high-tech murderous costume. "This stuff is garbage. I was killing guys like this ten years ago with my bare hands. This is a sport of death and honor, the code of the gladiators."

Once again, Jesse's performance worked. Obviously, he was typecast in the role; an over-the-top non-athlete athlete with a flair for entertaining macho glibness—clad in a Lycra uniform from the reject bin of the Hall of Justice—it was no stretch. Nonetheless, he more than held his own alongside other jock actors, like Jim Brown, and seemed to be a Hollywood comer. His salary quadrupled to $20,000 a week.

He and Schwarzenegger continued their practical-joke-filled, slightly competitive budding friendship. A few days into filming, Jesse figured out that Schwarzenegger would wake up early to work out each morning. Jesse set his alarm so he could beat Schwarzenegger to the gym, and before Ah-nuld arrived, he soaked himself with water giving the appearance that he'd been strenuously pumping iron for hours.

"We're going to have to start getting up earlier," Schwarzenegger said to his trainer, " 'cause it appears that Jesse is much more serious than I am."

Surprisingly, Jesse's acting career never took off as these earlier projects might have otherwise indicated. He was always eager for new work, occasionally traveling to LA to try to drum up offers, but the roles—especially for characters like Blain or Captain Freedom—weren't coming as fast as his performance in *Predator* might have indicated. He played a sports commentator in *No Holds Barred*, Hulk Hogan's truly awful pro wrestling vehicle, and alongside Okerlund in *Repossessed*, a 1990 horror movie spoof starring Leslie Nielsen and Linda Blair the viewing of which may make you embarrassed on behalf of all multicelled organisms. In 1989 Jesse appeared in *Thunderground*, an independent movie that doesn't appear in many comprehensive movie encyclopedias. He played a villain, worked for three days, and was paid $25,000.

"I just don't think he got the kind of roles he really wanted or had hoped for," says Pitt, who soon no longer was representing Jesse. "Sometimes there are no answers for why that happens. There are no reasons. Maybe the roles aren't there, or the actor becomes distracted by doing something else and changes his focus—which he clearly did."

"Some guys are like stars, and some guys are character guys," Burch says. "Jesse is more of a character."

In 1989, however, Jesse did get a chance to finally star in a movie. His one and only starring role. Unfortunately for him—as well as for the rest of humanity—the result was *Abraxas, Guardian of the Universe.*

Damian Lee is one of those Hollywood types who wears a number of hats—producer, writer, director, actor—and has been in any number of pictures, most of them modest both in terms of critical acclaim and budget. A Canadian ski racer who'd appeared on ABC's *Wild World of Sports*, Lee first segued into film in 1983, as writer, producer, and an actor in *Copper Mountain*, which starred Alan Thicke, former congressional spouse/*Playboy* model Rita Jenrette, and a very young, very green Jim Carrey.

Lee had met Jesse through the various players in what he calls the "Munich Muscle Mafia." Bodybuilder Franco Columbo had come to the set of another picture Lee was working on—*Circle Man*—to help the star of the film get his weight under control. Lee and Columbo hit it off, and since Columbo was close friends with Schwarzenegger—and best man at his wedding—Lee also met Lou Pitt, agent to Schwarzenegger and, soon enough, Jesse.

When Lee was putting together the film *Thunderground*, he thought of Jesse. The movie—which Lee likens to *Paper Moon*—features a young female hobo traveling the country with a male counterpart who ekes out a living through the occasional barefisted fight. The climax of the heretofore forgotten picture features a "mythical character, an extremely idiosyncratic man—called 'The Man'—who will fight you for any bet—whatever sum you choose," Lee says. The Man was played by Jesse, as Lee was looking for "an incredibly wealthy, completely eccentric and bizarre character . . . a character you'd see in the WWF."

"I identify with that role perfectly," Jesse said, "because I am an eccentric, and I am a maniac."[35]

Thunderground came and went, however, and soon Lee was looking for a leading man for his next movie. He felt the character of Abraxas called for "a wrestling-type persona: a strong, big, heroic-looking individual. Jesse is certainly that, if nothing else."

The character of Abraxas is an alien cop who comes to our planet to capture an evil alien who has impregnated an Earth woman with a mutant embryo. "I thought Jesse's countenance would be interesting to play an alien on Earth," Lee says. "It's sort of a role based on the book *A Stranger in a Strange Land*, and Jesse has a lovely, almost innocent quality at times."

Lee thought the combination of Jesse's intimidating bulk with his beneath-the-surface, occasionally naive sweetness would make him perfect for Abraxas, for whom "everything seems quite extraordinary taken at face value."

With Pitt representing him, Jesse agreed to the part and was paid about $250,000. "For someone who was really cutting his teeth—and this was his first leading role," Lee says that Jesse's salary, while nowhere near Schwarzenegger dollars, was more than adequate compensation. "A lot of actors sweat blood and mortgage their houses to get their first opportunity," he says.

Filming began in central Ontario in November, 1989, in a small town called Thornbury two hours northeast of Toronto and right on the Georgian Bay. Lee immediately thought he'd made the right decision in casting Jesse. "He has the right persona for that kind of noble and honorable-type hero," he says. "And he's very good with kids and there's a very large child factor in the movie as well."

Additionally, Jesse "took direction well"—not a small plus for an actor from a director's perspective, especially considering the filming conditions for Abraxas.

"We did this picture in rather unusual circumstances," Toronto native Lee says. "It was very, very cold. One night it was thirty below zero. And it was windy." Considering that many of Jesse's scenes were shot with him dressed in light clothing, Lee says that the experience was a "real test of mettle"—a test that the former Navy SEAL passed with flying colors, though it wreaked havoc on his health and kept him out of the Buccaneers broadcasting booth for a few weeks. "It was a tough shoot," Lee says. And not just the fourteen-hour Canadian nights when much of the shooting took place.

For some of the scenes, Jesse had to stand dressed in skimpy clothing, outdoors, and in water. "The water was cold enough to induce hypothermia," Lee says. "We had to cut holes in the ice for him. . . . there was a physical threat of a very real nature." It's impossible to know what got Jesse to actually take the plunge—his machismo, the money, the potential of fame for his first starring role, or just the fact that he had agreed to do so—but he did.

"Damian," Jesse said, as he marched toward the lake, "I'm not going in this water."

"Jess, I think that's a good idea," Lee replied. Jesse kept walking.

"I'm not going in," he'd repeat.

"Good idea, Jess," returned Lee. "It's too cold today."

Then he'd march right into the water and Lee would yell "Action!"

It would be difficult to argue that the resultant film was worth Jesse risking even just the sniffles for, much less his health.

The story begins when evil alien Secundus impregnates an Earth girl, Sonia Murray, whose baby will have impossibly destructive capabilities. Abraxas, a "Finder"—essentially a space cop—is sent to earth to capture Secundus, his former partner, and teleport him back to intergalactic jail, a task he disposes with rather quickly. But when Abraxas's bosses tell him to kill the impregnated Sonia before she can give birth, he balks at the task. Sonia delivers within minutes, thus assuring that both Secundus and Abraxas will return to earth.

Secundus escapes from space jail five years later and returns to Earth to unleash Tommy's "anti-life equation." Secundus tracks down both Sonia and Tommy in a small Canadian town, and attempts to overload

Tommy's "mind with fear and confusion" until the anti-life equation spills out, which will render Secundus omnipotent. Tommy has yet to speak a word, which complicates matters.

Abraxas is sent down to kill Tommy before Secundus can get the equation, but Abraxas—who has a conscience, unlike his supervisors at interspace cop HQ—spends the duration of the film disobeying orders, trying instead to kill Secundus and protect both Tommy and his mother, with whom he quickly falls in love. Meanwhile, Secundus leaves a trail of bodies in his wake.

Jesse plays the title character, an 11,862-year-old alien virgin cop with a clear sense of right and wrong. His co-stars are Sven-Ole Thorsen and Marjorie Bransfield. Thorsen, a Denmark-born stuntman and bit player from *The Running Man* and various other Schwarzenegger flicks, assumed the role of the evil Secundus. Bransfield, who looks like a young version of Arkansas cabaret singer Gennifer Flowers, was a frequent cast member in almost every single film featuring Jim Belushi. In this one, however, as "Sonia," she was the lead, and *Belushi* the bit player—Belushi shows up inexplicably in the first half of the movie in a brief scene seemingly ad-libbed.

In almost every possible way, *Abraxas* is horrendous. The script is stilted and clichéd, the special effects are cheap, and the acting is laughably unconvincing. Thorsen speaks with Schwarzenegger's accent, but that's where the comparison ends. Though Bransfield's world is rocked by aliens—her son's life is created and then threatened by one of them—she never emotes more than your average housecat. It almost makes you wonder what a spectacular talent like Jim Belushi is doing in such a picture.

Jesse's performance is fairly bad, but by no means is it the weakest link in the chain. There are glimmers of a certain credible tenderness, but generally his performance is wooden and bogus. His on-screen kiss of Bransfield is particularly rigid and uninspired; even the fight scenes are unsatisfying. The film doesn't sink to the level of so-bad-it's-good, but rather hovers in a gray zone of just plain awful.

"You know, I think I'm going to like living here," Abraxas says after zapping Secundus at the end of the film. "This planet has a great deal of potential," he adds as he walks off into the sunset with his new family, Sonia and Tommy—who finally speaks.

Oscar-winners or not, the cast and crew of *Abraxas* had fun while filming, according to Lee. Jesse and his co-stars were housed in some idyllic condos on the Georgian Bay, and they all enjoyed each other's company. They were like-minded sub-stars, hustling for fame and cash, hoping for the best but suspecting that their third-tier status wasn't going to be shed anytime soon.

"It was an interesting and odd bundle of goodfellas," says Lee. The cast didn't exactly blend in with Thornbury's 1,400 residents. Thornbury "is a very Scottish-Irish salt-of-the-earth type place," Lee says. "Thornbury's main street is two blocks long, and all the buildings were built by these Bible-fearing Presbyterians." It was an odd disconnect for Lee to see his actors in this setting.

Pro wrestling enjoys a huge Canadian fan base, so Jesse was already a star in Thornbury. "Jesse melded in very well with the local people and was very patient with them," Lee says. "He certainly took his time signing autographs and posing for pictures."

Like the people of Thornbury, Lee found Jesse to

have "a real salt-of-the-earth quality to him," and was taken with Jesse's closeness with his family when they visited him during shooting. "There is really no hidden agenda to Jesse," Lee says. "What you see is what you get."

SEVEN

MAYOR VENTURA

Jim, Terry, Ty, and Jade had moved to Brooklyn Park—the sixth largest city in the state—in 1983. Tucked ten miles northwest of the Twin Cities, and on the west bank of the Mississippi River, Brooklyn Park offered the Venturas the blend of the City's urbaneness with the parks and trails and green life of a populous countryside. With a 1990 population of slightly more than 56,000, and more than 1,500 acres of park land, Brooklyn Park felt small. But it was growing.

Because it was growing, and so quickly, the mayor of Brooklyn Park needed to be the kind of person who could help the city grow responsibly. In 1983, Jim Krautkremer was that mayor.

Krautkremer liked to plan. He planned professionally, helping to manage a computer operation for the Minneapolis-based Fortune 500 company Midland Co-operatives, Inc. Krautkremer thought he could use his skills to help out Brooklyn Park, where he and his wife Shirley were raising their four kids. In '68 he won a seat on the city's planning commission. He got elected to city council soon after, when another city councilman decided not to run for re-election.

Krautkremer was not one for confrontation—he only ran for mayor of Brooklyn Park in '72 because—as with his city council seat—the incumbent had de-

cided not to run. And, as Krautkremer explains it,
"People said, 'Why don't you run?' and I did. But I
probably would not have run if the mayor had run
again."

Under his watch, Brooklyn Park soon earned a national reputation for planning and controlling development. Krautkremer wore his wonkish achievement
like a Purple Heart.

"We were one of the first communities in the state
to develop a comprehensive plan to develop," he
brags, as a member of the planning commission that
recommended that plan and the city councilman who
voted it through. "Planning is something I felt
strongly about," he says. It was necessary "when
you're working with computers . . . to make sure that
things fit the needs of today and the future." He notes
that the Y2K computer problem is a result of bad planning.

Brooklyn Park couldn't afford bad planning. It was
a fast-growing community—16,000 residents when he
took his first oath of office as mayor, and 56,000 eighteen years later, when he left. During his tenure,
Krautkremer organized the umbrella group—Brooklyn
park Community Organizations (BPCO)—an organization of organizations. BPCO helped return some of
the spunk of the Brooklyn Park "Tater Daze" festival.
Krautkremer also represented Brooklyn Park on the
Metropolitan Council, which served Minneapolis, St.
Paul, and the seven-county area. He slaved away on
the Council's transportation advisory board, as well as
other committees, for years. He also served on the
board and as president of the Association of Metropolitan Municipalities.

The people of Brooklyn Park rewarded Jim Krautkremer for his hard work, for his skills and love for

planning. They kept re-electing him, every two years. Then the charter was changed and they re-elected him every four years. It went like this for almost a generation, from 1972 until 1990.

But there's one thing—possibly only one thing—that Jim Krautkremer had never planned on. And that was having to face off against Jesse "The Body" Ventura.

Jesse has described the epiphanous incident in rather simplistic and shaded terms. "It started over the fight for environment, a wetland," he told C-SPAN. "The city wanted to come in and destroy this nice, beautiful wetland in our neighborhood for no apparent reason . . . We lived in a very older, rural part of town, had a rural look to it. Nobody had a water problem. There was no need for it."

But the truth is somewhat more complex—and illuminating, in terms of the kinds of issues that motivate Jesse to action. For almost half a decade, Jesse paid the city government no attention—often not even voting—until a property dispute came to him. It was nothing abnormal, just one of those Not-In-My-Backyard arguments so common to civic debates. In late 1987, a wetland area on Brooklyn Park's West River Road was slated for development and the neighbors were riled up. The neighborhood, on the banks of the Mississippi River, was home to some of the most expensive homes in the area, Jesse and Terry Ventura's among them.

Krautkremer says his hands were tied. "This developer came in and wanted to develop the land," he says. He owned it and had every right to build on it—"We were trying to get him to do some planning when he put it together so he would take care of his drainage problems and also make sure that it was more than just throwing up more problems. He was willing to work with us. And we did have meetings with the people in the neighborhood.''

The developers ''certainly did have the right to build on it,'' says Joe Enge, one of the neighbors leading the charge against the development. ''However, there were certain regulations . . . and we didn't feel that the city, typically being the final say over what happens, was really keeping a watchful eye for the environment.''

Mayor Krautkremer, however, doubted the genuineness of the residents' concern for the environment. ''I don't think it was the wetland,'' he says today. ''It was the development people didn't want in their neighborhood.'' That was the bottom line, Krautkremer thought. Some of the development's opponents ''had a strong feeling for the environment,'' but most of them just ''used the wetland as a way of getting people involved.''

Enge and the neighborhood activists tried to fight City Hall in every way they knew how. They urged the city to buy the property. It was adjacent to a neighborhood park, and not far from an elementary school. Certainly keeping the wetland and its surrounding area free of clutter was preferable to the multi-family townhomes or the small apartment complex the city was about to allow.

''The owner of the land could have put up anything as long as it met with the minimum ordinances,'' Krautkremer argues. ''But he was willing to work with us.'' The residents, however, weren't so cooperative, at least not according to the view from Krautkremer's chair. ''We came up with a definite plan that would have upgraded the park, held up the wetland, and homes''—not on but near the wetland—''would have been put up in good manner. And still then, the people did not want it.''

Enge and his fellow activists took a petition around, getting 450 signatures opposed to the project. ''But after all was said and done,'' Enge says, the City Council ''voted seven to zero against us.''

Enge and his crew—including Jesse—couldn't believe the arrogance of the city government. Who *were* these people? Who on earth *elected* them? Weren't they supposed to serve *the people*? Wasn't that their *job*?

At this point, West River Road resident Jesse Ventura jumped into the public debate.

''If you don't respond or listen to us,'' Jesse said ''like the [Warren Zevon] song, you'd better 'send lawyers, guns and money, 'cause the shit has hit the fan.' ''

Though he didn't know it at the time, Jesse had delivered his first political speech—one infinitely consistent with his future political rhetoric.

In November, 1988, Enge ran for a seat on the City Council. Jesse was one of Enge's campaign chairpersons. Brooklyn Park candidates don't run as members of a party, they just run as individuals—but the political lines of ''old'' and ''new'' were clearly delineated.

''When I ran, the intent that I had . . . was that I would be the first—but certainly there was more to follow,'' Enge says. The Minnesota born-and-bred stockbroker—and Brooklyn Park's newest City Councilman, as of November 1988—immediately began urging Jesse to run for Mayor.

''The first time I was aware that there even was a Ventura,'' recalls former Mayor Krautkremer, ''was when somebody kept interrupting the meeting. When

I ran a council meeting, I tried to make sure that everyone there . . . [got] a chance to talk. Someone kept interrupting and finally I gaveled him down and said,
'just a minute!'

"One of the councilmen said, 'Do you know who
that was?'

"I said 'No.' I think at the time (Jesse) had red-
and-green hair."

"So the councilman said, 'He's Jesse Ventura!'

"And I said, 'Who's that?' "

Krautkremer would know soon enough.

It had been a bad year for Jesse. In August 1990, he
and Vince Jr. got into a huge fight and Vince Jr. fired
him, just like that.

That was it, in a split second, no more microphone,
no more banter with "Gah-RIL-lah," no more place
for Jesse in wrestling.

The fight between these two headstrong and ambi-
tious men was, of course, over money. According to
Jesse's testimony, his suspicions of Vince Jr.'s tactics
had begun early on. He had been excited to join the
WWF, but in 1985, right before he got into the ring
one night in Milwaukee, Monsoon—who was also a
WWF executive—handed Jesse a contract and told
him he had to sign it or he couldn't wrestle. Jesse
signed it, but he told Monsoon that he was only doing
so under duress.

Then after the first *WrestleMania*, Jesse found out
that Matt Borne had made more for his mid-card bout
wrestling Ricky Steamboat—maybe ten minutes'
work—than Jesse had made doing his schtick for three
hours.

Vince Jr. didn't have his best interests at heart,
Jesse thought. When he told him he'd been given the

part in *Predator,* Vince Jr.'s reaction was to yell at him.

"Who's the agent?!" Vince Jr. yelled.

"Barry Bloom," Jesse said.

"Tell him he's fired!" Vince Jr. commanded.[36]

"How do you fire him when he doesn't work for you, Vince?" Jesse asked. Vince Jr. told Jesse that he and the WWF could hook him up with a much better agent than Bloom.

"Mr. McMahon," Jesse said, "if you hire the agent, the agent is not going to be working for me. He's going to be working for you and he's going to have your best interests in mind, not necessarily mine. No thank you. I'll stick with Mr. Bloom."

Vince Jr. kept yelling and yelling. He didn't calm down until Jesse said, "Am I speaking with Vince McMahon or Verne Gagne?"

Then in the late eighties, after Jesse started receiving royalty checks from various merchandise associated with *Predator* and *The Running Man*, he started to wonder why WWF wasn't cutting him similar checks for the continued use of his image. He wasn't salaried, after all, and Vince Jr. was making millions off Jesse's image—video games, Topps trading cards, videos of wrestling events. Jesse and Bloom had asked for a cut. Vince had said no. It went back and forth for years.

They were in the midst of settling on a figure in 1990 when Jesse sold his image to Sega-Genesis for $40,000 for use in a video game. Vince Jr. was infuriated—WWF had a deal with Nintendo which he thought should preclude Jesse's deal. Neither man would blink.

Buy out my Sega contract if you're so worried, Jesse told Vince Jr. But Vince Jr. said no.

He said more than that, actually. "If you do this, Jesse, your job is in jeopardy," he threatened.[37]

But Jesse took the deal. "Vince, I signed this Sega thing," he told his boss. "I guess you have to do what you got to do."

For his part, Vince Jr. thought Jesse had an unbelievably overinflated ego. Jesse wasn't the main event at the *Main Events*—he was just an announcer! Jesse—and his agent, Barry Bloom—had been a pain in the ass ever since Jesse got back from filming *Predator* in Mexico in '86. Richard Glover, who represented the WWF in its negotiations with Bloom, later testified that Vince Jr. thought that Jesse's requests were "blatantly outrageous," that Jesse was "wasting [the WWF's] time even trying to negotiate, because things on the other side, he felt, were quite unreasonable."[38]

So, even though Jesse had just signed a contract with WWF earlier that year, in August 1990, Vince Jr. fired Jesse.

Jesse was filled with rage. Mayor Krautkremer happened to be in the way.

Out of frustration, Jesse had told Krautkremer at one of the meetings, "You're gonna make me run against you, aren't you?"

"I said, 'Well, that's your right, but I have a responsibility' to run an orderly government," Krautkremer says. But he didn't take seriously any threat of opposition from some pro wrestler barely involved with the community. One of Krautkremer's friends called out to Jesse, "You can't win!"

You don't tell a SEAL he can't do something, Jesse thought.

Jesse had stayed in touch with Freeman "Mac" McInroy, his old high-school teacher who'd always told him to get involved. One day he came down to a pep rally and approached Mac. He told Mac about the development and the arrogance of Krautkremer and the rest.

"He told me he was getting tired of it," Mac recalls.

"Well, Coach," Jesse said to him. "I'm gonna go get my name on the petition and I'm gonna run for office."

"Well, great," Mac said. "Do it! That's the way you get things done."

Jesse went and turned in a petition to run for mayor. Krautkremer was surprised—it wasn't that powerful a position, really—just a glorified city council seat, just one of seven votes. Plus a gavel for the meetings. It was only a part-time job, only paid about $900 a month.

Krautkremer wasn't used to any real competition. He ran a modest family campaign; his wife and kids helped him screen-print his campaign signs, while he himself prepared his flyers. "I knew that this election was going to be difficult," he says.

Vince Jr. had fired him, so Jesse had time, after all. Time and anger. Times like this Terry would call him a warrior. No, this wasn't a good year to get in Jesse's way.

Jesse's campaign "had a well-organized group, I give him credit for that," says Rick Engh, a Brooklyn Park resident of thirty-five years, former Brooklyn Park cop, and fourteen-year city councilman. "He had a person—who was on the city council before—who did a super job keeping track of anyone who had a gripe with the city council. And when it came time for Jesse to run, Jesse talked to all of the people who were upset—and evidently that was the swing vote."

Like anti-development activist Enge before him,

Jesse ran against the "Old Boy's Network" he said was running Brooklyn Park unwisely and unaccountably. "Together, we can build a partnership of residents, city employees, and officials—and improve our city's image ourselves, instead of 'buying' a better image through public relations consultants," read some of his campaign literature.

He was still very much Jesse "The Body," however: "A political campaign is like a war without guns," he brayed to the local newspaper, the Brooklyn Park *Sun Post*, in a 1990 interview. His memory of the wetland debate was still fresh in his mind. "I saw how frustrating it can be when residents go to a city council, and they're so condescending, all the decisions have already been made," he said in an interview with *USA Today*. "It doesn't matter how many citizens don't want it . . . My slogan is I'm going to give the neighborhoods back to the neighbors."

Krautkremer was worried—and concerned. Jesse didn't even bother to show up for their one scheduled debate at the community center. He might win this thing just on name ID alone, and the guy didn't even care enough to come to the debate!

And when Jesse did bother to participate, Krautkremer resented some of his tactics. "We had a murder in the area," he recalls, "and they tried to make that into an issue of law and order, saying that we had been unresponsive." That wasn't fair, Krautkremer thought. The city council had been adding policemen to the force.

Jesse also made issues of things Krautkremer thought petty: he promised to cancel a proposal to build a new $4 million city hall; he said he would open lines of communication between the city council and the citizenry; he wanted to broadcast all city council meetings on local cable access. "You know I love performing for the camera," he repeatedly said throughout his campaign.

Jesse had a core group of volunteers, most gleaned from the wetland group. They knocked on doors and papered the town with leaflets.

In 1987, 2,632 Brooklyn Park voters had turned out to vote. In 1990, for Jesse's mayoral campaign, the rolls swelled to 20,118.

Hoo-yah!

Some of the increased turnout can be attributed to high-profile statewide races for governor and senate. But much of it can also be attributed to Jesse's energetic, highly publicized campaign. When voting booths closed that November night, Jesse had carried all 21 of the city's precincts, scoring 12,728 votes. Krautkremer had only managed 7,390.

WCCO radio hosts Eric Eskola and Mark Ginther tracked Jesse and Terry down at Brooklyn Park City Hall at around 2:30 that morning.

"I can't believe you won," Ginther said.

"No, neither can I," Terry laughed. She put Jesse on the phone.

Eskola, a big wrestling fan, started ribbing Jesse. "So, Jesse, who are you going to assign to be head of the streets department? 'Nature Boy' Ric Flair?" Eskola asked.

"Hey, this is real serious stuff," Jesse said. "I'm really into this, I really have a strong belief in trying to do a good job for the community."

"I was impressed with that," Ginther says. "Instead of just complaining, he was willing to step in there and actually try to improve things."

Early the next morning, "Mac" McInroy walked into Roosevelt High School.

"Mr. McInroy," a secretary said, "there's a guy with a real gruff voice on the phone. You gotta come get this call."

"Hello?" Mac said.

"Well, Coach, I've done it," said the husky voice on the other end of the line. "I am now the mayor. They gotta come in and see me."

Krautkremer tried to be a gentleman, a good loser. He met with Mayor Ventura at the clubhouse at the golf course and congratulated him.

"Because of your name, you can do much more for the community in four years than I've done over a longer period of time," he said.

But, perhaps not surprisingly, Krautkremer holds a dim view of Mayor Ventura's term. "I told him he could become an important part of the community," he says. "But I don't think he did that."

There is a world of difference between campaigning and governing. Especially for Jesse, whose campaign had been based on fighting the "old boys' network" members of city council who still retained a 5–2 majority. It was a very rocky four years.

"Primarily, the reason there was a lot of head butting is because he and I ran against a political machine," says Enge, Mayor Ventura's one ally on the city council during the first half of his term. "They were used to doing things the way they had been doing them. There was a sense that we had that a lot of deals that got done were maybe to benefit a few people. It was made no secret when I ran and when he ran that we were going to be putting an end to those deals, and we wanted people to be accountable. So I don't think we got a positive reception from the people who were in office with that message."

On January 14, 1991, Mayor Ventura's first meeting as mayor, he and Enge were on the losing end of the first of many 5–2 votes. "The stage is set, isn't it?" Jesse said.[39]

Jesse's message wasn't the only quality that undercut his ability to get along with the long-time members of the city council. He was still "The Body," showing up for his first meeting in a sportscoat and tee-shirt, a black bandanna tied around his bald head. Sitting beneath a portrait of George Washington, he seemed more than a little out of place—and when he spoke, that impression was reinforced even more so. The sounds and speeches of Mayor Ventura were far from the temperate, fence-sitting cautiousness that so many Americans were growing sick of. Many people found him refreshingly honest.

Weeks later, for instance, the U.S. Congress would abide by a request from then-President George Bush and authorize use of force against Iraq. As a new political voice—and a Vietnam veteran at that—Jesse's bluntly honest assessment of the Gulf War situation was quoted throughout the nation. One month after Desert Storm was launched, *USA Today* interviewed him alongside a former Air Force major general, and Middle East studies experts from UC-Berkeley and the Center for Middle Eastern Studies.

"Saddam Hussein is a tyrant, but he's our Frankenstein," Jesse said. "We created him with good intentions, but the monster got worse and worse until he was out of control."

In November, Jesse appeared alongside a more mixed sampling of Americans for a *Newsweek* temperature-taking. Again, his response was remarkable for its refreshing candor:

"Emotionally, I was for sending the troops at the beginning. But as time has gone on—and I've learned more—I'm for withdrawal. What happened to Kuwait was a tragedy, but my heart is telling me as a Vietnam vet that we don't need 50,000 of our young men to die over there. I'm afraid it's a tragedy waiting to happen. And I wonder if Big Business and Big Oil aren't behind it. OPEC is holding the world hostage. Let's explore oil opportunities elsewhere. It's an atrocity that our young men should die to protect oil barons. We have internal problems that are just as important as the problems in Kuwait.''[40]

Mayor Ventura's takes on the War in the Gulf were hardly the sounds of an experienced politician—they sound more like what a friend or cool uncle might tell you over a beer. But Jesse's crudely open analyses worked for precisely that very reason. The next year, presidential candidate H. Ross Perot would earn about 20% of the national vote appealing to the voters' tangible need to hear such straight talk. Jesse was developing this skill as well.

Not every Brooklyn Parker took a similar shine to Jesse's tenor and tone, of course. He continued to strut and preen, running around town in a black baseball cap that read ''Vietnam—We were winning when I left.'' Some people ate it up, loved the schtick. Others didn't.

''I didn't like how he treated the public,'' says former city councilman Engh, who served as mayor pro tempe, presiding over meetings whenever Jesse wasn't around. ''When he got elected, he came over to my house and said, 'You're gonna do things my way.' And I said, 'Waitaminute, here!' He said, 'Do you want to be mayor pro tempe?!' ''

Engh explained to the new mayor that the position of mayor pro tempe wasn't a mayoral appointment but rather a decision left up to the rest of council, usually given to whoever had served the longest. "Then he stormed out," Engh recalls.

"He was a professional intimidator," says ten-year city council member Ron Dow, who lived in Brooklyn Park for thirty-seven years. "If he didn't know something, he was very aggressive. If you spoke in opposition to what he wanted done, he got very upset, very easily . . . If [citizens at public meetings] spoke against what he wanted, he cut them short."

Dow and other Ventura critics thought that the Mayor was all show and no substance—and they didn't even particularly like the show.

"He tends to simplify issues when he doesn't understand them," Dow says. "He acts like, 'Oh, we can do this—that's no problem.' But if things got too deep, he got very defensive.

"One time I made some mention about wrestling and about violence on TV," Dow recalls. "I think a lot of kids today have learned a lot from watching professional wrestling, and they don't respect authority anymore—like wrestlers do not respect referees, they're always hiding a two-by-four in their shorts . . . I've seen my grandson clothesline a kid on a bicycle. I've seen him try things after a wrestling match on his little sister. So I spoke against the violence that wrestling teaches kids."

Jesse was not pleased.

"I was not supposed to bring up his private life— he got very, very upset," Dow says. "I was walking out and he came up to me and said, 'I want to take you outside. Come on, let's you and me go outside and straighten this out.'

"I'm a hell of a lot older than him, and a lot smaller than him," Dow says. He turned down the invitation.

"Jesse's a flamboyant showman with a short fuse,"

says Harvey Rockwood, managing editor of the news-paper group that ran the Brooklyn Park *Sun Post* at the time. "He was very thin-skinned . . . He wanted the press to roll over and play dead."

Jesse's critics say that he treated most of the city's management personnel in a gruff and arrogant manner, if not actually calling them out. "I think in the back of his mind he may have thought that "These are the Good Old Boys, and we're gonna throw all the Good Old Boys out," guesses Engh.

Jesse made life particularly difficult for city manager Craig Rapp. One winter night in '92, Mayor Ventura allowed two hours of public comment on Rapp's performance. Though Rapp had been endorsed by the council, he later said he felt like quitting after listening to citizen upon citizen rag on him for everyone to hear, in Jesse's interesting version of Open Mike Night. Jesse argued that it was all in the name of increased accountability and communication, but to Rapp it felt like plain old meanness.

Another fight Jesse picked was over the city's ownership of the Edinburgh U.S.A. Golf Course's Clubhouse. According to Jesse ally Enge, the venture stank from the get-go. A group of local businessmen had lost around $800,000 in just two years in the endeavor. Jesse had a philosophical problem with the city running what he felt should be left to the private sector, but he got really steamed when the head businessman—Alan Anderson—asked and received a 43% raise. In a May 1993 emergency council meeting, Jesse had told the chamber that two telephone callers told him that Anderson was "a pathological liar" and would "rob from you." Anderson later sued Jesse for defaming him at that meeting, but a judge dismissed the case.

Anderson's company, however, was investigated for the alleged misuse of approximately $15,000 of Clubhouse funds. No evidence of illegal activities was found—though the city's accountant did find his business guilty of sloppy bookkeeping and city manager Rapp did not renew his contract.

"To me, this vindicates everything I've been fighting for," Jesse told the Minneapolis *Star Tribune*.

One of Jesse's indisputable accomplishments was to increase voter participation and interest in local government.

Though she'd lived in Brooklyn Park for almost forty years, Grace Arbogast, for instance, had never been even remotely interested in politics. She was active in the community, sure—a volunteer for the Fireman's Auxiliary, a member of the Mrs. Jaycess, a girls softball coach. But politics didn't interest her. She was busy with her job with the insurance company, and tied up with family and home responsibilities.

In the beginning months of 1992, city planners started to talk about widening the street where Arbogast and her family lived, Sixty-third Avenue. The sidewalk they were talking about building would take down some of her forty-year-old evergreen trees! They wanted to turn her garage around so that it spilled onto a different street altogether! Arbogast didn't want this, didn't want this at all.

Jesse had "opened up city government to the people," Arbogast remembers. "People started to come more to meetings and to express their opinions on various subjects in the city." Arbogast was one of them. Upset about the government's plans for her evergreens and her garage, she marched right down to City Hall to tell them why their plans for Sixty-third Avenue were wrong.

She found Jesse unusually receptive to her plight. He would listen to her. He would walk up and down Sixty-third Avenue, talking to neighbors about what they wanted. Before the council came to a vote, Jesse said he needed a few minutes before he could make a final decision.

"I'm gonna walk it one more time," he said. It was a cold day, but he turned down a neighbor's offer for a lift. No, he needed to soak it up and knock on a few doors.

"He talked with all the neighbors and came to an agreement," Arbogast says. "We worked all the differences out. We came to a win-win solution." Arbogast thought Jesse was "very much in touch with the people."

Then "the people"—or more specifically, her neighbors—started urging Arbogast to run herself. She went to Jesse and Enge to find out what that entailed. They liked Arbogast, thought she'd be another independent voice on the City Council. They offered their support. They endorsed her. Jesse even went door-to-door for her, drumming up votes.

In November 1992, Arbogast won, defeating Rick Engh. Jesse was still in the minority, but at least now it was 4–3.

But the proverbial good old boys were going to fight back. As part of his mayorly duties, Jesse served on the city's Economic Development Authority (EDA) office—a seven-member body made up of council members. After the Anderson fracas, as a direct slap in Jesse's face, on February 8, 1993, EDA members voted council member Robert Stromberg president instead of Jesse. Four days later, Jesse resigned from the

EDA altogether—even though the City Charter prohibits the mayor from resigning.

In addition to his genuine animus, there was another reason for the Mayor's tough-guy demeanor: Jesse loved to perform. But the skills he had picked up in pro wrestling and Hollywood didn't really lend themselves to the previously serene settings of Brooklyn Park civic debates.

At one council meeting in March, 1993, Jesse was absent—not an infrequent occurrence—when councilman Stromberg made a motion to appoint a new member of a police commission. Jesse's ally Enge pointed out that only the mayor had the authority to make that appointment. Stromberg withdrew his motion. When Jesse returned to council chambers a week later, however, he decided to make a point, the purpose of which was more theatrical than anything else.

"[It] came to my attention last week that a motion was made to move forward on [the nomination to the police commission]," Jesse said, "and I felt that that concerns me greatly because I am the mayor, and it's my job to do that, Mr. Stromberg."

"And we took it back right away, by the way," Stromberg said, "We didn't—"

"Well, you know . . . I'm very upset over the fact that it seems that you four are always trying to loop around me lately, and I was elected by the people to serve as mayor. You are not, sir. I am the mayor. You are now president of the EDA because you and three other people up here decided to make you president of the EDA. I'm going to give you a quote, face-to-face, eye-to-eye. The quote comes from the former world heavyweight champion, 'Nature Boy' Ric Flair."

"Never heard of him," Stromberg said.

"Well, fine," Jesse responded. 'But the quote is, "If you want to be the man, you got to beat the man.' "

"Mr. Mayor," Stromberg protested, "I'm not into—"

"You're not mayor yet, Mr. Stromberg," Jesse said.

"I am not into intimidation," Stromberg said, "or standing nose-to-nose and trying to punch it out with somebody—"

"Neither am I," said Jesse.

"—but that's exactly what you're doing right now," Stromberg rejoined. "It's about the silliest thing I've ever seen."

"But it's entertaining to the folks at home," Jesse said.

"We're not here for entertainment," said Stromberg. "I'm sorry."

"I am,"[41] said Jesse.

The *Sun Post* didn't approve of Jesse's over-the-top theatrics that day, and they made that clear in an editorial as well as a transcript of the exchange with Stromberg. "He was very angry about that," says managing editor Rockwood. Jesse stormed into the office, gave the editorial writer a piece of his mind, and then stomped out, where he ran into Rockwood smoking a cigarette.

"Hey, Jesse," Rockwood said. "What's going on?"

"Your newspaper said I was shit!" Jesse said.

"What?!" Rockwood asked.

"Your newspaper said I was shit!" Jesse repeated.

"I thought he was joking," Rockwood recalls. "I couldn't imagine that he was serious. 'Look, go back in there and find the edition of the paper where it says that you were shit,' " Rockwood said. "But that was the wrong thing to say. He came back to me, and he walked over with his finger wagging and right up in my face. I got terribly uneasy. I thought he might be getting ready to haul off and punch me." Rockwood excused himself and returned to his desk.

As Mayor, Jesse preached a libertarian philosophy— less government, fewer taxes, more individual liberties. But a closer examination of his mayoral career belies an inconsistency in his views that borders on hypocrisy.

During a council debate about liquor licenses, Jesse waxed free-market, suggesting that liquor sales should be no more restricted than the sale of Twinkies. Jesse also supported the use of marijuana for therapeutic purposes even going so far as to say that his opposition to the narcotic would be hypocritical. (Jesse has acknowledged smoking marijuana in the past.) These positions are perfectly consistent with the opinion of libertarians like William F. Buckley, who has long advocated the legalization of drugs.

But almost in the same breath, however, in 1992 Jesse proposed an ordinance restricting the open sale of tobacco products at checkout counters—since they posed too much of a "temptation."

Jesse had long opposed the tobacco industry, having cut a number of anti-smoking TV ads in 1985 for the Minnesota Department of Health. "I'm Jesse The Body, and I've been smoke-free all of my life,"[42] he said. Later that same year, Jesse also participated in an anti-smoking concert with the Soldiers of Fortune.

His opposition to tobacco products was a personal one. In the first few years of his wrestling career, Jesse began dipping Copenhagen Snuff. In the early 1990s,

his nearly-twenty-year habit manifested itself by forming a lesion inside his lip, one that his dentist told him
could cause him to lose a third of his face. Jesse swore
he'd quit. But it wasn't so easy. He'd stop by the con-
venience store on an errand, and right there by the cash
register, the tiny tins of Copenhagen would sit, taunting him. Sweat would begin to pour from his brow.
His hands would start to shake.

From his personal struggle came his proposal to ban
tobacco ads and hide tobacco products in Brooklyn
Park retail food outlets. After he announced the proposal, Jesse's office was besieged with tobacco lobbyists, and the ordinance eventually died.

That this one opposition to this issue of individual
liberty stemmed from Jesse's own personal difficulties
can be seen as admirable—a willingness to try to help
the rest of society from a lesson learned through his
own weakness. But Jesse's shortsightedness on issues
that he could not personally relate to would be a trend
that would follow him throughout his political career.
A career that began, one might observe, because Jesse
didn't want a developer to build on property he had
every right to build on—because it was on Jesse's
street.

It was all part of a pattern of unfairness, say Jesse's
Brooklyn Park opponents. He would let his supporters
speak at hearings for hours, "but if you disagreed with
him he'd try to cut you off, or argue with you, or make
fun of you," says Ron Dow. "He was unfair through
the whole political process."

His opponents would argue that Jesse's mayoral
term was marked by clear moments when he tried to
bully his opponents, and skirt the rules, playing fast-
and-loose with the facts like the politicians his father—
and, later, he himself—would love to demonize.

It was only because Jesse remained in the minority for his entire term that taxes went up every year he was mayor, he says. By the end of his four years, he was able to point to a few solid achievements other than just opening city council meetings to a television camera for local cable access.

In '91, Jesse went to Washington, D.C., to try to loosen Federal coffers to fund a highway artery through Brooklyn Park known as 610. He returned with $36 million, "surprising [his constituents] with his lobbying skills," according to *Governing* Magazine. Even his political enemies gave him some credit for that, though they balked when there was talk of naming part of 610 "Ventura Highway." Jesse, however, liked the idea. "I think it would be hilarious," he said.

One of the ways Jesse helped secure the multi-million dollar Federal funding was by greasing a few palms. Along with the mayors of two other local suburbs, Jesse brought more than $5,000 in campaign donations from local businessmen for the congressmen they were meeting with.

He was particularly proud of reducing crime, he would say as his term came to a close. While the crime rate went down both nationally and statewide, Jesse took credit for Brooklyn Park's share. When naysayers gave credit for the reduced crime rate to area police, who increased patrols, Jesse would say, "And who the hell do you think went in and told them to boost the patrols up? I was the one who went riding along with the cops."[43]

This is Jesse bluster at its most egregious. Without question, Jesse was supportive of the efforts of the Brooklyn Park Police Department. But so was every other mayor and member of city council, says Don

Davis, Chief of Police for the city from 1978 until 1993. The downward trend in crime "began prior to his coming in as mayor," Davis says, and was largely due to the force's adoption of community-oriented policing techniques, which began in 1988. "We went from no community groups to now there are almost 200," Davis says. Brooklyn Park's efforts were so successful, in fact, Governor Arne Carlson tapped Davis to be the state's commissioner of public safety.

The increased number of officers on the street also played a large factor. During Jesse's reign, the population of Brooklyn Park increased from approximately 57,500 in 1991 to around 60,500 in 1994—or about 5%. In that time, the number of sworn officers on the Brooklyn Park Police Department increased as well, from fifty-eight to sixty-seven—a 15% increase. Increased visibility of officers on the street tends to lower the rate of crimes like aggravated assault, robbery, and auto theft. The number of incidents of those crimes—according to Lee Glamm, crime prevention specialist for the BPPD—plummeted during the years of Jesse's reign.

According to Glamm, Brooklyn Park crime stats didn't even universally decrease during Jesse's term. From the beginning to the end of Jesse's mayoral term, for instance, incidents of reported rape increased as much as almost 100%—from twenty-three in 1991 to forty-five in 1994. There was one homicide in Brooklyn Park in the year Jesse ran for mayor—which Krautkremer says Jesse's campaign crassly used against him—but there were two in 1992 and four in 1993. As with most crime statistics, says Glamm, "it was kind of a mixed bag."

Clearly, however, "Jesse was supportive of police endeavors," according to former chief Davis, who notes that Jesse in particular "liked programs for kids." Davis recalls that the city council was urging him to have his officers participate in the DARE program, encouraging kids to stay off drugs. Davis pointed out that his department didn't have the resources to hire two extra officers to lecture the kids, much less to fly the two officers to the DARE training in Illinois or California.

"I got more frequent-flier miles than I know what to do with," Jesse said, offering his tickets to the BPPD. They ended up not needing them, but Davis was nonetheless impressed with Jesse's offer.

The one indisputably valid criticism of Jesse's first foray into politics concerns his almost offensively high rate of absenteeism. Even ally Enge concedes that "he did miss a lot of meetings," though he adds that "it's not as big of an issue that they want to make it. When there were issues of importance, . . . he did make sure to make it back."

Jesse's absentee rate was just one of the ugly and petty squabbles of Brooklyn Park politics during the Jesse era. It may have seemed like a silly point to bring up—especially for the part-time job of mayor of a small town most Americans have never even heard of. Still, Jesse himself had made the grab for the steering wheel, brushing aside an eighteen-year incumbent to do so. It probably wasn't unreasonable to ask that he show up for the job.

But Jesse's energies during that time were stretched thin—in acting, wrestling announcing, football broadcasting, and talk radio. He hustled to keep his name in print, his face on the air, his name in conversation. Being Mayor of Brooklyn Park was just one of the many balls he had in the air.

With one of these jobs, as a talk radio shock jock

The WWF Years–Jesse "The Body" Ventura in a photo taken from the WWF's "The Wrestling Album" in 1985. (Associated Press Photos)

1986–Jesse "The Body" with entertainer/vixen Elvira. (Associated Press Photos/File)

Jesse in a promotional still from the 1987 science fiction film *Predator*. (20th Century Fox/Archive Photos)

1991–Jesse Ventura, Mayor, Brooklyn Park, Minnesota. (Mark Weygand/Reflex)

October 1998–Ventura has his head powdered before the taping of a debate in St. Paul, Minnesota. (Associated Press Photos/Jim Mone)

January 4, 1999–Jesse Ventura is sworn in as the thirty-seventh governor of Minnesota in a ceremony at the Minnesota State Capitol in St. Paul. From left, his wife Terry, daughter Jade, and son Tyrel surround him. (Associated Press Photos/Ann Heisenfelt)

Famous friends like Arnold Schwarzenegger wish him well on his first day as governor.
(Associated Press Photos/Richard Marshall, Pool)

Making further Hollywood connections, Jesse Ventura appears on *The Tonight Show* with Jay Leno. (Associated Press Photos/Chris Pizzello)

for local station KSTP, he did manage to accomplish something that met his political ends. "He'd regularly come in on Wednesday morning and start ripping on the [*Sun Post*] for 'inaccuracies,' " reports former managing editor Rockwood. But Jesse's definition for what constituted an inaccuracy seemed rather wide. "If you quoted somebody that had a different opinion from him on an issue, he'd consider that an inaccuracy," Rockwood says.

Jesse also used his forum at KSTP to repeatedly dis Stromberg, who was defeated three to one in the 1994 nonpartisan mayoral primary by Arbogast, whose candidacy he trumpeted. He bad-mouthed her November opponent as well. And, of course, she won.

Jesse's outside work from the beginning of his mayoral term, in 1990, up to his run for the governor's seat in 1998, reveals a lot about the man—in terms of where his passions were fading (pro wrestling), where they were growing (political speechifyin'), and where they remained the same (bombast and childlike need for attention). He was evolving, finding something of a purpose.

By June 14, 1994, when Jesse announced that he would not run for reelection, it seemed clear that his greatest achievement as Mayor was serving as the strongest shock to an entrenched, staid, and possibly arrogant political system.

"I rode into town, I ran the bad guys out of town, and now it's time for me to ride into the sunset with a hearty 'Hi-yo, Silver,' " he said to any reporter within earshot. And while calling Krautkremer, Engh, Dow, and the others "bad guys" may be a taffy-pull of a stretch, Jesse did, unquestionably, breathe new life into a dull suburban political body—and increase community involvement and interest as well. In 1994, his allies Enge and Arbogast became members of the majority. The previously apolitical Arbogast, in fact, was elected mayor.

But right before he could deliver his "Hi-yo Silver!" cheer, Jesse would make one more attempt to sneak around the rules, delivering an issue—however silly—right into the hands of his political enemies.

Jesse and his wife called it "Jester's Falling Tree Ranch"—"Jester" being a mixture of Jesse and Terry. A $500,000 thirty-two-acre ranch off Brockton Lane North in Maple Grove, a nearby suburb, "Jester's Falling Tree Ranch" was the Venturas' dreamhouse, a place where Terry could raise and breed her horses—which she had been boarding at great expense. There was room there for Ty, for Jade ... even for Bernice Janos, Jesse's mother, who was ailing and on her own ever since George had died in 1991.

They bought it on June 1, 1994, and soon put up a sign outside, "Fine quality pleasure and show horses" They added a $20,000 swimming pool.

None of these niceties mattered much to Stromberg. That the Mayor of Brooklyn Park—even a lame duck with only four months left in his term—that he would be so arrogant as to actually move out of the city he supposedly ran ... Why, the gall! The unmitigated gall!

Why, it was clear that he didn't live in Brooklyn Park anymore, wasn't it? His house on West River Road had been listed for sale with a real estate company since July 18. The city charter said that the mayor had to live in Brooklyn Park. State law said so, too. Just because he still *owned* the house on West River Road didn't mean anything ... it certainly didn't mean residency, in any case.

Stromberg got people talking. If they asked Jesse,

he'd show them his driver's license, which listed Brooklyn Park as his home city. If they asked him where he slept, he'd be coy—maybe on his Harley, he'd say.

As if it wasn't enough that the guy was absent for almost half the meetings—about 40% by his count, Stromberg would explain. "In my opinion, this appears to be a direct violation of the city charter, and I want to ask the council to make a full investigation."[44]

It got ugly. Where did Jesse live? He ducked all queries.

"Answer the question, Jesse," blared an editorial headline in the *Sun Post*. In the end, the local paper had concluded that Jesse had been a decent mayor. Crime went down, new business had come in. "That's not to say he was the only person responsible for the turnaround," the paper said, "but as Mayor, he helped bring about the changes."

Still, the question persisted—where did he live? Had he really been so arrogant, so callous and indifferent, to leave before his term was up?

"During Ventura's mayoral campaign, he promised to have an open, responsive government," the *Sun Post* reminded him. "To quote his campaign literature, 'Residents should be able to go to City Hall and ask questions and get prompt, honest answers.'

"Well, Jesse," the newspaper concluded, "the people are asking."

Stromberg was asking the most loudly, however. It reached a shrill yell at a summer 1994 city council meeting where Stromberg successfully—though narrowly—fought off an effort to have the state auditor investigate whether Stromberg had abused his position by having the city remove a hedge from his property at taxpayers' expense.

"Mr. Mayor, I really have some questions about you ripping off the city," Stromberg said. He pointed out that the Mayor had missed twenty-one out of fifty-two meetings in '93. "You can go and attack all you want, but when someone comes back you don't have the guts to take it."[45]

Jesse was furious, and his face was flush with anger. "I'm taking it," he said. "I will allow you to continue, to show that I have the guts to look you in the eye."

How could Jesse claim Brooklyn Park residency? Stromberg asked. His mail was being forward to the Maple Grove ranch home as of July 8, the house was vacant and up for grabs, Ty and Jade had transferred to another school district. The Venturas' *cable* had been cancelled, for Godssake!

Jesse was getting desperate. It seemed that he just didn't want to admit the truth, to come clean with the fact that he left town a little early, no big deal, right? But apologies didn't come quick to Jesse, especially not when backed into a corner. He grabbed at the nearest straw—the illusion of the unknowable, personal, explanation.

"You don't know my personal situation," Jesse said. "How do you know my wife and I haven't separated?"

He wouldn't back down. Not to Stromberg, that's for damn sure. He got shifty, slippery even. He filled out a new change of address card, re-forwarding his mail back to his Brooklyn Park abode. He re-enrolled Ty and Jade in the Brooklyn Park school district.

On September 21, the song-and-dance about where Jesse lived grew to a theater of the absurd as he was forced to testify before an administrative law judge to determine where he truly lived.

"They were just trying to put a cloud over him and over any candidate he endorsed," Enge says. "By doing that, they hoped their side could get power and keep power from shifting."

It caused a stink, sure, but in the end, Jesse's side won. The judge ruled in his favor—even recommending that the city reimburse him for legal fees.

EIGHT

THE DRIFTER

The season after the Buccaneers kicked Jesse out of their broadcast booth, he was plucked up by the Minnesota Vikings. Sitting alongside play-by-play announcer Dan Rowe and analyst Dave Huffman—a former Viking lineman—Jesse was hired as an experiment by the general manager of Minneapolis's KFAN radio. He was a well-known local boy who made good, at that point in his first year as Mayor of Brooklyn Park.

"He offered kind of a glorified fan's appraisal of the game as it went along," Rowe says. "His value to the whole picture was that he didn't mince any words."

He hit it off with the Vikings. Uninhibited in the presence of the football players, he would approach them boldly—unlike many deferential sports reporters—and could even talk about weightlifting with some of the bigger guys. After Jesse had shaved his head bald—except for a small tail from the back of his head—he took some ribbing on the team plane as they flew back from Tampa Bay. Jesse was wandering the aisles, chatting up the players with characteristic confidence, when Huffman got on the plane's loudspeaker and, introducing himself as the captain in his official-sounding voice, asked if the "Hare Krishna" walking around the plane would please sit down. Jesse smiled sheepishly and returned to his seat as the plane erupted in laughter.

In the booth the three-man tag-team didn't work as well in Minnesota, unfortunately. The chemistry that Jesse had enjoyed with "Big" Al and "Mean" Gene just wasn't there. "It was difficult for all three of us to say something after every play," Rowe explains. "We only had so many seconds."

There were other problems, too. At first, Rowe says that Jesse's boundless energy was a distraction. "People still see—when they're around Jesse for any length of time—he rocks in his chair. Back and forth, and back and forth, and back and forth. After a while, peripherally, you get used to it. But at first it was pretty distracting . . . Some people would have to take Dramamine" to keep their composure, Rowe jokes.

Rowe mentions that during the few discussions he had with Jesse on away games, he was impressed with the retired athlete's knowledge of current events. "Before I even knew him, I just thought he was some old wrestler that didn't have a lot going on—but I was amazed by his depth."

Rowe wouldn't have time to get to know Jesse much better. After the Vikings' rather mediocre season ended in 1992, word came down from up top: Three men in the booth was proving to be just too many. Jesse got a call. They were sorry. But it just wasn't working out.

What to do, what to do . . . ? The WWF wasn't going to be calling Jesse anytime this millennium, *that* was for damn sure. In 1991, Jesse had filed a lawsuit against Vince Jr. and the WWF, demanding a percentage of the cash they had made and were continuing to make off his image. The civil case, heard by

U.S. District Court judge Paul Magnuson, dragged on for a few years. Motions were filed. Depositions were taken. Countermotions and challenges and analysis of the controlling law.

As the case continued, Jesse's belief that he'd been screwed was only reinforced. The WWF had led Bloom to believe that Jesse wasn't alone, that no one received royalties. But as early as 1986, Hogan had been gleaning 5% of the take from sales of a video-cassette in which he appeared.

Even a fraction of Hogan's generous deal would add up to some serious bucks! The WWF's parent company, Titan, and its business partners had sold more than $25 million in videotapes on which Jesse appeared, $2 million of Jesse dolls, $144,000 worth of '87 and '88 calendars featuring Jesse's likeness as both a WWF announcer and in *Predator*, $730,000 worth of computer games, $2.4 million of trading cards and God-knows-how-much in T-shirts and other souvenirs.

On July 21, 1994, Judge Magnuson ruled that the WWF was to pay Jesse $809,958.66. He was also to get $85,568.20 in prejudgement interest, and $66.57 per day from April 21, 1994, until the WWF coughed it up.

Victory!

Hooyah!

Even though the WWF bridge had been burned, in 1992, Jesse got another opportunity to announce in the world of pro wrestling. It would be his last.

The wheels had been set in motion back in the late eighties, when in a pinch Atlanta-based mogul Ted Turner bought a wrestling league. Wrestling had been a staple of the programming menu for his Superstation WTBS, but the league he'd been using was about to go belly-up. So to Turner it made perfect sense to buy his own wrestling outfit for TBS. In 1988, he purchased the National Wrestling Alliance in Charlotte, North Carolina, the WWF's strongest competitor, and changed its name to World Championship Wrestling (WCW).

Things didn't pick up for a while—many people in the wrestling world thought that Turner just had no idea what to do or how to market it. He replaced the man running WCW with Kip Frey. Some say that Frey knew much more.

In early 1992, Frey offered Jesse a fat contract— $950,000 for two years—thinking that the announcer would help bring WCW an audience. "Frey thought that Jesse was a bigger celebrity than almost all the wrestlers," *Wrestling Observer Newsletter*'s David Meltzer says.

Jesse thought so, too. "It's like the history of pro football. What did the AFL do? It hired Joe Namath,"[46] Jesse crowed.

But wrestling fans didn't necessarily share Jesse's inflated view of his importance to the sport. Jesse was certainly no Namath—he didn't wrestle anymore, hadn't really starred in a hyped match in at least five years. Jesse wasn't even a Howard Cosell; he was more like another Minnesota native, John Madden— something of a marquee name, someone whose commentary fans enjoyed, though he occasionally crept into a caricature of himself and too much of him could grow old fast.

"When he showed up for WCW," says Meltzer, "the knock on him was that he thought he was the star. But nobody ever bought a pay-per-view event to see Jesse announce."

For WWF fans, Jesse had been an entertaining part

of the show, no question. But it wasn't as if the WWF's ratings had gone down since Vince Jr. canned his ass two years before. "He was a very popular television announcer," Meltzer says. "But in the war between the two sides, as far as being a significant force, he wasn't at all." In fact, Meltzer points out, 1993—the first full year Jesse announced for the WCW—was the organization's worst year ever. "It was the bottom of the barrel . . . they averaged maybe 960 fans a show."

Frey lasted only four months before being replaced by Bill Watts. By 1994, WCW had picked up Hulk Hogan and noted wrestling promoter Zane Bresloff, and the company began its turnaround. Watts reportedly was disappointed to have been stuck honoring Jesse's sizable contract, which he had viewed as too generous. Still, he honored it.

The job of a wrestling announcer was changing, and increasingly a color man's *raison d'être* was to move the product of pro wrestling: an announcer was to tell and hype the rivalries and the feuds, accentuate the good points of each wrestler, explain to viewers why it was so important to buy tickets to the next event when it came to their city, and urge fans to buy the company's next pay-per-view event.

Jesse had a different idea, though—to entertain, and to hype himself. Watts, a former wrestling promoter, didn't think Jesse was doing enough to help to move the product. He and Jesse locked horns more than a few times.

"He always wanted to do things his way," says Okerlund. "And he would upset a lot of people. They'd say, 'You can't work with the guy.'" Though Okerlund likes Jesse, he says that "there are a lot of announcers and producers and wrestlers that Jesse offended," mainly with his ego.

Jesse's announcing also began to suffer from an inescapable phenomenon to which we all eventually succumb: the irrelevance that comes with age. Starting in the early nineties, new wrestlers were coming in— from other countries, especially—and changing the sport. The show put on by the Calgary Japanese was more high-flying, with less posturing and posing. The action of the sport was increasing dramatically, meaning there was less time before head-thumping, less space for Jesse's jokes and persona.

Jesse and other announcers weren't as familiar with the new aspects of the sport—"fans were ahead of the announcers," Meltzer says. "What the announcers knew just wasn't relevant anymore. And at the end, Jesse just lost a lot of interest, I think." (Other announcers would fall victim to becoming anachronistic, including Vince Jr., who took himself out in 1997.)

Hardcore wrestling fans started complaining about Jesse—in Meltzer's newsletter, fans no longer voted Jesse one of the "best announcers" in 1993 or 1994, a category he won throughout the late eighties.

Eric Bischoff took Watts's job in '94, and began to lead WCW to the prominence it enjoys today. That year, former Bad Guy pro wrestling manager Bobby "The Brain" Heenan was brought in to announce a few events while Jesse was on vacation. "Immediately (Heenan's) work was better," Meltzer says.

Bischoff preferred Heenan, too. By the summer, Heenan would announce eight or nine bouts in an event, while Jesse would get only one. "Jesse just pouted on the air," Meltzer says. "He made it very clear that he was upset only doing one."

Wrestling insiders began to refer to Jesse as "Wally Pipp." Yankee first baseman Pipp had called in sick one day and so Lou Gehrig filled in for him—and never stopped starting for the next 16 years. Pipp quickly fell into the Where Are They Now? files.

Jesse wasn't trying anymore. His feud with Watts had demoralized him, and then when Heenan "Pipp"ed him, he just gave up. Bischoff paid out the last six months on Jesse's contract, but didn't use him.

"Jesse got disinterested with announcing and his job performance fell off," says a WCW executive. "There's no doubt that he had talent, but it became real obvious—as far as his doing his homework, being prepared for the job, and his enthusiasm—that his job performance went down, and we parted ways."

"You can't make wrestling react to you, you have to react to it," Meltzer says. "It's a constantly changing sport."

The momentum of Jesse's Hollywood career was on a similar, indisputably downward trajectory. He played "Chewalski" in the Joel Silver-produced *Ricochet*, an action film released in 1991 starring Denzel Washington and John Lithgow. But his character only existed to be a prison tough guy Lithgow could beat up and kill.

In September 1991, Jesse began co-starring on a short-lived syndicated show called *Grudge Match*. The show—which Jesse called "a combination of 'Double Dare' and 'Judge Wapner' "[47]—was lowbrow dreck at its absolute basest level. In each hour-long episode, two contenders were given the opportunity to settle whatever score existed between them with weapons like spaghetti, pudding, or oversized boxing gloves. Michael Buffer, of "Let's Get Ready to Ruuuuuuumble!" fame, was the ring announcer; John Pinette, the rotund comedian who was mugged in the final episode of *Seinfeld*, served as the wacky ref; and Jesse provided color commentary.

"Well, Michael," Jesse said to the loser of one *Grudge Match*, who duked it out with his buddy with cream pies because he'd been stuck talking to "the ugly girl" while they were out trolling—"You lost in the bar when you lost the girl. Unfortunately you lost here on *The Grudge Match*. My sympathy goes out for you, but is any girl really worth this?"[48]

Mercifully, the show didn't last very long.

Though he was listed twelfth in the opening credits of 1993's *Demolition Man*—produced by Joel Silver and starring Sylvester Stallone and Wesley Snipes in a twenty-first-century cops and robbers thriller—he appeared before the camera an hour and a half into the picture, for only seconds, and had no lines. His parts were shrinking. (Notably, the film features a satiric reference to a future Schwarzenegger presidency, perhaps not as comically impossible as may have been thought during filming.)

His movie roles required him to do little more than be big and look menacing. Like the dancing dwarf from *Twin Peaks*, or the obese mama from *What's Eating Gilbert Grape?*, Jesse was cast only for his physique and menacing scowl. He spoke on-screen infrequently. He was "White Lightning" in *Major League II* (1994) and appeared that same year in an episode of the TV talk show *Vicki,* sitting with other pro wrestlers, including Johnny B. Badd and "Ravishing" Rick Rude.

He was grasping at straws. In 1995, Jesse became the spokesman for Pig's Eye Beer. That year he also appeared at the Computer Sales and Products Exposition, held in the education building of the Minnesota State Fair Grounds on behalf of Combat Connection—

a "dedicated game server supporting up to ninety-six lines of interactive game play." He was an anonymous, cartoony, unnamed "Man in Black" in a 1996 episode of *The X-Files*.

By the time of his last movie, *Batman and Robin*, which featured Schwarzenegger as bad-guy Mr. Freeze, Jesse's film career had officially devolved: from break-out co-star with a promising future to bit player whose character doesn't even have a name. As a guard at Gotham City's Arkham Asylum for the Criminally Insane, Jesse appears in two scenes—one in which he imprisons Mr. Freeze, and the other in which he is killed during Freeze's escape. He is listed thirty-seventh in the closing credits, behind Vermont Senator Patrick Leahy, who had a cameo as himself.

Things weren't exactly looking up for his Hollywood career.

NINE

THE JESSE VENTURA SHOW

One morning in 1991, Brooklyn Park grade-schooler Ty Ventura phoned up a local radio station. Ty's pop was, by then, a fairly well-known Minnesota celeb, so someone at the station thought it'd be funny to put Ty on the air, introducing him as Tyrel "The Boy" Ventura. It became a recurring bit.

"It really wasn't even that funny of a segment," says Steve Konrad, the producer. "We just liked saying the name."

In January '92, Konrad began working as program director at KSTP-AM, a talk radio station in the St. Paul suburb of Maplewood. In December, Konrad phoned up Jesse at the Brooklyn Park City Hall and left a voice-mail message for him. Konrad knew that Jesse was a colorful guy and had "lived a hell of a life and therefore was qualified to discuss that on the radio."

Talk radio was fast becoming one of the most successful trends in radio history, as well as serving an influential role in nineties-era politics. While there were only 300 or so news/talk radio stations in the country at the end of the 1980s, that number had swelled to more than a thousand only a few years later. Led by hosts Howard Stern, Rush Limbaugh, Don Imus, and G. Gordon Liddy, 70% of these talk radio hosts were politically conservative, and more than 80% of them were men, according to *Washington Post* media critic Howard Kurtz's study of the phenomenon in *Hot Air: All Talk All the Time*.

That the unpolished Jesse Ventura would be considered for a talk radio show wasn't as unusual as it may seem. One of talk radio's very appeals was its rawness. "In a world of blow-dried commentators with carefully modulated opinions," Kurtz wrote, "radio talkmeisters [had] rough edges."

That Jesse was, as Mayor of Brooklyn Park, also a politician didn't matter. Jason Lewis, another talk radio host on KSTP, had once run for congress, as had Don Imus. Ollie North and Pat Buchanan would run back and forth between their roles as jabbers and candidates, and out-of-work politicians Ed Koch (and soon enough, Mario Cuomo) could also find employment pontificating to a radio audience. Even Howard Stern had once seriously contemplated a gubernatorial run in New York, as a Libertarian.

Jesse called Konrad back immediately. They met for lunch.

"At that point I was just thinking of fill-in work," Konrad says. "But he was an interesting guy, and I wanted to put interesting people on the radio. Three lunches later we had a morning show."

The "Jesse Ventura Show" started in January 1993, running from 5:30 until 9:00 each weekday morning. It took a while for Jesse to adapt to the format, to fill the daunting volume of minutes he had to fill. "It was a little rough at first," Konrad says. "Talk radio is very different from doing wrestling commentary, it's very different from doing football announcing. For the first several months, it was the Jesse 900 number—'Call me and talk to Jesse,' " Konrad says,

launching into a fairly impressive Ventura impression.
The ratings were in the basement.

After several months, Jesse grew more comfortable
with the format. Talk radio was enjoying a conver-
gence with the "Angry-White-Men" zeitgeist of '93
and '94 that would both fuel and reflect the November
1994 Republican revolution, and Jesse, once again,
was in the right place at the right time, marketing himself in the right way.

"He was getting better about the same time as the
Republican landslide of '94," Konrad says. "It sort of
coincided." This helped Jesse—whose weakness as a
talk radio host was generating material. "There was a
lot of material that just kind of happened," Konrad
says. "A lot of stories were going on that were very
consistent with his interests, so he didn't have to generate material, he could react."

David Ruth, an afternoon producer at the station in
his mid-twenties was brought on board to help Jesse,
and the show started to hit its stride. "If there was a
topic and he could work in some sort of public policy
angle, that's the kind of show he would do," Ruth
says. "Jesse's really good at formulating his opinions
and getting them across to the public—but he needs a
person or people around him to help him package
them."

Ruth would come in at around 3:30 in the morning,
read the papers and the Internet, watch the previous
night's news, and write a page full of possible topics
for his boss to discuss.

"He came in with ideas, too," Ruth says. Topics-
of-the-day included gun control—which Jesse opposed—and other legislation which he felt intruded on
individual rights and personal liberties. He also took
some time to settle some Brooklyn Park-era scores,

waging war against the mayoral campaign of his Brooklyn Park enemy Stromberg, and on behalf of his ally Arbogast.

He also settled an even older score, says "Mean" Gene Okerlund. In 1995, Hulk Hogan had come under fire for an alleged incident of sexual harassment. "When [WCW] came to town for an event in the spring of 1996, Jesse just badgered the hell out of Hogan for two days on his radio show. "Jesse was brutal," Okerlund recalls. "And he had quite a forum to air his gripes. For that reason, Hogan has relayed to me that he has no intention of returning to Minnesota. 'I'd just as soon not work the town,' he said."

Jesse had eighteen hours a week to fill, so anything and everything that occurred to him got mentioned— except for his family, which he seldom mentioned at all. "If you ever want to get him going, ask him about that JFK–Lee Harvey Oswald deal," Konrad says, alluding to Jesse's predilection for conspiracy theories about the Kennedy assassination. Jesse talked about the Vikings, the Timberwolves, his days as a SEAL, his pro wrestling experiences, his work in films.

He even talked about the soap opera he'd been watching since his pro wrestling days on the road, *The Young and the Restless*. Konrad heard Jesse riffing about the show, and thought it was hilarious to watch the immense macho man delving into the ridiculous plot points of the soap. From time to time, Konrad would have Ruth play the soap's theme song and Jesse would deliver a plot synopsis. " 'Oh, deres Vic—he's da man—and he wants so-and-so,' " Konrad says, imitating Jesse. " 'And den dere's his ex-wife, and she wants him back, but she's too chicken to say nuttin'.' "

As is fairly common on talk-radio stations, Jesse

enjoyed a joking rivalry with several of the other
hosts. He was always plugging that he knew Schwarzenegger, and when the immense Austrian was in the
Twin Cities area filming *Jingle All the Way*, there
wasn't a news organization in the area that wasn't trying to score an interview with the superstar. Several
of Jesse's colleagues at KSTP took the opportunity to
insinuate that Jesse's claim to friendship with Schwarzenegger was bogus. But on the film's last day of
shooting, they were all stunned when Schwarzenegger
actually called up and talked to Jesse on the air for
about 15 minutes. "Afterwards, he said, 'Now, you be
sure to tell Joe Soucheray,' " Konrad says, mentioning
the afternoon host who had been casting doubt on the
reality of the friendship.

Jesse would also playfully squabble with Barbara
Carlson, the moderate Republican whose show followed his, and had a passionate though friendly rivalry
with Jason Lewis, the right-wing host who was on
from six to nine PM.

"Everybody liked him," Konrad says. "The guy is
just such a giant bag of pure charisma. Everywhere
that he went . . . people were just clamoring to get near
him. They just wanted to touch him, to talk to him, to
hang out with him." KSTP's hosts all participated in
a St. Paul Winter Carnival Parade, and Jesse "easily
had more people screaming for him than the whole
rest of our staff combined," Konrad says. Throughout
it all, Konrad was amazed at the warmth and friend-
liness Jesse showed his admiring public—and his hu-
mility. "He was as normal and average a guy you
could hang around with."

A goo-goo eyed intern asked Jesse about pro wrestling one time, Ruth remembers. Was it fake?

"Come here, Dave," Jesse said to Ruth. He

grabbed his young producer and "put me in a move, I think it was called 'The Sugar,' " Ruth recalls.

"Does this look fake?" Jesse asked the intern.

"He likes having a good time," Ruth says.

Jesse hated commercial breaks—they interrupted the momentum of his riffs. A fidgeting mass of energy, he would leave the booth between commercials and corner unsuspecting KSTP staff members so he could continue spewing forth—"He'd want to keep talking about whatever it was he'd been talking about," Konrad says. "During a commercial break he'd come out to the office and if there was somebody there he'd talk to them about it—it didn't matter if it was an intern or somebody touring the office, he'd talk your ear off," adds Ruth. Even after the show, Jesse was frequently spotted immediately outside the building holding court on a variety of subjects.

"Jesse does a radio show on the air, and he does a radio show off the air," says Ruth.

Jesse sometimes went too far. In 1995, liberal Minnesota State Representative Myron Orfield—upset about the squalor in some Twin Cities neighborhoods—drafted a bill which would have attempted to ease the disparity in property tax revenues between the inner city and more prosperous suburbs. Orfield was respected nationally. "He has invented, or he has popularized and given intellectual support to, a very important innovation in the politics of regionalism," a senior fellow at the Brookings Institution in Washington, D.C., said of Orfield to National Public Radio. The Minnesota state house passed Orfield's bill, but Republican Governor Arne Carlson vetoed it. There were thoughtful arguments on each side of the issue.

Jesse's were not among them. On May 5, he called Orfield a "Communist" on his radio show. Orfield wrote to the station complaining about Jesse's attack; the station invited Orfield onto the show, an invitation Orfield accepted. On the program, Jesse kept referring to Orfield as a "Communist." Orfield thought the talk-show host's behavior not only appalling and Mc-Carthyite, but possibly defamatory.

The next day, Jesse corrected himself, changing his label for Orfield to a "Socialist." He continued to attack Orfield and his bill. Orfield phoned up, but kept getting put on hold.

"This type of talk radio warps public debate," Orfield wrote in a letter to the editor of the *Star Tribune*. "It is geared to create anger, not public discussion. If you are to be unlucky enough to be attacked unfairly, there is no possibility of redress. If you respond, they attack you harder. They control access. It is like arguing with an opponent who has a big black tar brush. Whatever you say, they just smack you with tar." Orfield wrote that Ventura and his KSTP colleague Jason Lewis, who had also been attacking him, were "preying on the weak and lonely of our society in a way that is very similar to the broadcaster Father Coughlin and other radio demagogues of the past. These demagogues had a deeply detrimental effect on the political process. In a fair public policy debate, both sides should have access."

But talk radio is far more like pro wrestling than it is to a "fair public policy debate"—the sides are uneven, the outcome is fixed, and enemies are demonized.

"It's my show and I can do what I want," Jesse said. "Who said I had to be responsible?"[49]

According to Orfield, Jesse's remarks were all the more infuriating not only because the lower-middle class angry white males who listened to talk radio were likely to benefit from his bill's tax-base shifting, but because Jesse had previously supported fiscal disparities sharing as Mayor of Brooklyn Park. This made sense—Brooklyn Park at that time had been the area's largest per-household recipient of the fiscal disparities system. But Jesse was no longer Mayor of Brooklyn Park, he was a talk radio host in an era of right-wing rhetoric.

"Wrestling is like talk radio—I might say things just to stir up emotions, and it might not be what I really think,"[50] Jesse would say.

Others say that Orfield got as good as he gave. "Myron's sort of a troublemaker on his own," says Steven Schier, chairman of Carleton College's political science department and a political analyst for KSTP-TV. "He's always trying to bring up these unpopular subjects—and bring them up in the public arena—so it's not a surprise to me that those two would butt heads."

Mostly, though, Jesse's public policy debates were innocuous—and even fun. In July, 1995, when a Minneapolis engineer sent a memo to city workers warning them that they would be disciplined for ogling women—which he called "visual harassment"—Jesse was all over it.

"I got a problem with that," Jesse said on the air. "How on earth can they discipline people for looking?" He said that he knew women who used their lunch hour to ogle men. Government interference in people's lives, ogling chicks ... a topic perfect for Jesse's show.

" 'Ogling by de construction workers, what's wrong wit' dat?' " Konrad says, throwing out another Jesse impression.

However much Konrad and others in KSTP management liked Jesse personally, however, radio is a tenuous business and by mid-1996, the honchos at KSTP were still unhappy with Jesse's show. He was still having problems providing material. Ratings had gone up, then, after the Republic revolution peaked, they started a downward slide in 1995.

"I heard him in the early days," says Okerlund. "I was a nine-year radio veteran. Trust me, this guy would never be able to get on the air" had he not been a celebrity.

Management had tried to tinker with Jesse's show, hiring a woman to do the news so she could throw subjects Jesse's way and creating a Howard Stern–Robin Quiversesque banter. But that didn't work. There was really one decision they were heading toward.

"It didn't work out in the end as what we'd hoped for," Konrad says. "It really wasn't working out from the standpoint of him providing his own topics. And listener interest had been fading off for more than a year."

In the summer of 1996, even though Jesse had just signed a two-year contract only five months beforehand, KSTP management told Jesse that he would soon be replaced. "They walked me in after a Thursday morning show," Jesse once said, "and the boss said, 'Well, we're taking our morning show in a new direction and it doesn't include you. You don't have to come in tomorrow.' "

Konrad maintains that the station wanted to keep Jesse on, maybe as a fill-in host. They wanted to work with him. "We weren't sure what that would mean, though," Konrad says.

Jesse took the news hard. He'd loved doing the show and hadn't seen the firing coming. He told Konrad he'd need a couple of days to think about staying with the station while relegated to a lesser role. He and Terry and the kids went to their lake home. Two days later, he told Konrad that he didn't feel comfortable hanging around the station after being replaced. It was one of the low points of Jesse's life.

"I feel bad about that," Konrad says. "That was not the intent from the radio station's standpoint. We probably did a lousy job of presenting to him that we still liked him and we still wanted him to be part of what we were doing."

Doug Westerman, the programming director for rival station KFAN, called Jesse up a few days after he was fired to see if he could fill in for some of his station's hosts. But Jesse told him that he had a "noncomplete" clause in his contract with KSTP which precluded his working for KFAN for some time.

He felt useless. He wandered around the house. He was unemployed for about a year. He volunteered as conditioning coach for Ty's football team at Champlin Park High School. Other than that he didn't really have much going on.

Another sad reality fueled Jesse's melancholy. In February, 1995, Bernice Janos died. She'd been ailing for a long time, and years before, she'd acquired atelectasis, a partial collapse of the lung. Her last few years were spent with Jesse and Terry and the kids. As her body was cremated and her ashes were scattered at her funeral in February, Jesse and Terry were heartbroken.

While Jesse was mired in sadness out at his ranch home, Westerman decided to put thoughts of hiring Jesse on hold until the "no compete" clause expired, in 1997.

That May, Westerman called up Bloom, Jesse's agent. From his brief discussion with the demoralized Jesse, Westerman knew that he didn't want to do morning radio anymore—the awake-by-3:30-AM-on-the-air-by-5:30 schedule had been tough for the forty-six-year-old. So Westerman made Bloom an offer—Jesse would get KFAN's mid-day show, from ten AM until one PM. KFAN even went so far as to hire David Ruth, who wasn't even in radio anymore. Negotiations continued through the summer.

In August, Westerman was close to the end of his rope. He'd been trying to get across to Bloom that KFAN management was firm with its offer. It was put up or shut up time for Jesse. If he didn't like the offer, that was it—he could walk away from the table. Westerman went away for a three-day weekend.

When he came back, there was a voice-mail message from Jesse.

" 'DOUG, IT'S JESSE VENTURA,' " Westerman recalls, launching into his own impersonation. " 'CALL ME AT HOME.' "

"Jesse was craving the spotlight—'cause he just loves to be in it," Westerman assesses. "So he wanted to make the deal work."

He did. Jesse started in August '97, and was an instant hit, bringing to KFAN his original following, and creating some new fans as well. He launched into similar themes. "Like the banning of personal watercraft," Ruth says, "that's the one that got him going from April through July. I had to beg him to stop talking about it." A bill before the Minnesota legislature would have banned personal watercraft on lakes smaller than 200 acres, a proposal Jesse couldn't abide as he loved his Wave Runner—on which he would tool around on a lake smaller than 200 acres.

Jesse had given up his Harley for the personal watercraft. "With those you can be far more daring and you can do wild things, and it can bring out in me what I need now and then to defy death," Jesse says. "I can do that and fall into the water and simply climb back on. You do that on a Harley and you get pavement burns. They're a lot more critical."[51]

The Wave Runner law was just the kind of idiotic meddling that government was becoming known for, Jesse thought. You go and find yourself a little patch of harmless fun and the Minnesota legislature has to come in and impose its nanny rules. As if those bozos had any idea what real danger was! Wave Runners were much safer than the way he used to get a danger fix, on his Harley. And even there the government had to go and impose its stupid helmet laws! It was all the same old bullshit from The Crips and The Bloods—his nicknames for the Democratic and Republican parties.

According to Ruth, however, Jesse's talk radio show took on plenty of issues—and not just those that affected Jesse personally. "He just hates the idea of banning anything," Ruth says. A local inventor had invented a mini camera to watch fish, and the legislature wanted to ban it for six months so it could discuss its impact. "Jesse's point was, 'Why ban something just so you can talk about it so you can find a reason to ban it?'" Ruth recalls.

"One day he came into work with this idea," Ruth recalls. "He said he wanted to ban the state legislature for two years—'cause they were banning everything else."

The same old unfettered, unpolished Jesse.

"Jesse just gets going and his grammar gets a little butchered sometimes," Westerman says. "His syntax

gets way out of whack." During one "personaliza-
tion"—when an announcer does an on-air plug for a
product—he would routinely botch the pronunciation
of "Spalon Montage," a Minneapolis spa/salon. The
Star Tribune's local gossip columnist, Cheryl Johnson,
devoted the lead graph a December 1997 column to
his clumsy tongue.

"I'm 'Jesse The Body,' I do what I want," Jesse
replied to Johnson. "You never followed me in wrestling. You've got to understand something. If 'Jesse
The Body' believes it, it is so. See? The persona I
created—he's never wrong."

Never one to pass up an opportunity at self-
promotion, Jesse then tried to convince Johnson to instead write about the fact that Terry's first colt bred at
Jester's Fallen Tree Ranch, "Show Me the Money,"
was named a Minnesota grand champion.[52] Johnson's
column mentioned "Show Me the Money," but also
included a phone number readers could call to hear
Jesse bumbling the name Spalon Montage; almost
3,000 readers called up to hear it.

Jesse's tin tongue sometimes irked his boss. An important part of radio is having the host continually say
the station's call letters and number, as well as the
specific name of the show and the host. "It has to do
with the ratings game," Westerman says. He kept trying to get Jesse to deliver the line—"Sports Leader,
AM 1130, KFAN, I'm Jesse Ventura." It was standard
practice, and important to the station, especially as the
show would segue from commercials back to the show
with a few riffs of what is called "bumper music."

But Jesse couldn't do it. He would come in out of
breaks, and he'd always have bumper music of Aeros-
mith or the Rolling Stones. But Jesse's formatics were
a radio programmer's nightmare. From a commercial

break, and Jesse would sing along with the bumper music and then just chime in with a statement indicating enthusiasm—but no call letters, no station ID, no name ID, even.

"'ALL RIIIIIIIGHT!'" Westerman imitates. "'HEY! YOU! GET OFFA MY CLOUD! ALL RIIIIGHT!' And then he'd go right into his topic. I really wanted the call letters mentioned, so I'd go and talk to him. He's easy to work with." But he just couldn't get it. Eventually Jesse developed something that went a little like, "'JESSE VENTURA! KFFFFFFFFFFAN!'" says Westerman. Eventually Westerman gave up.

As it had at KSTP, the radio show would follow Jesse around even when he wasn't on the air. He'd head out into the office during commercial breaks and—whether the person liked it or not—would engage bystanders in conversation. "Whoever it was, the person—out of courtesy—would listen: 'Yeah, Jesse . . . Yeah, Jesse . . .'" Westerman says. The poor victim would hear the bumper music and ask Jesse—"Don't you have to get back on the air?"

"OH YEAH, I DO!" Jesse would say, running back to the studio.

"After a while, as soon as people would hear the bumper music going into a commercial break," according to Westerman, "they'd scatter. Because they were busy. It's not that they didn't like him—they did. But he was like, 'I'm Jesse, and you're gonna listen to me when I talk!'"

He had more difficulty communicating when someone disagreed with him—someone on his own level. Once Jesse was involved in a heated discussion with Chad Hartman, another host at KFAN. "Jesse got loud and frustrated," Westerman recalls. Suddenly the whole newsroom could hear the last word: " 'HART-MAN!' " Jesse yelled. "WHY DON'T YOU GO FUCK YOURSELF?!' " Then he stormed out of the building.

He had a temper—there was no doubt about that. One day in 1998, rumors spread throughout the media about the demise of *Saturday Night Live* alumnus Phil Hartman, who had been killed by his wife. Jesse refused to talk about Hartman's death, and Ruth, his producer, didn't understand why. After all, Jesse had been perfectly willing to ramble on and on about the drug overdose of another *Saturday Night Live* alumnus, Chris Farley, which had occurred only a few months before. Ruth often chimed in on air with bits and comments, trying to help get his boss going, but Jesse refused to talk about it. Ruth found Jesse's reticence odd—and inconsistent.

"I called him a hypocrite," Ruth says. "When Phil Hartman got murdered, there was a day or two that we weren't sure about the facts, though it had been confirmed that he was dead. But Jesse would say that we weren't talking about it. Finally, at five minutes to one, I said, 'Boy, are you being a hypocrite, considering we talked about Farley.' He slammed the headphones down, and stormed away. 'You finish the show!' he said."

A couple days later, Jesse spoke with Ruth and explained his outburst. It turned out that Jesse had met Phil Hartman, and "he didn't want to ponder if he'd committed suicide, or if his wife had shot him." Once again, Jesse made an exception when an issue affected him personally. Ruth sees Jesse's temper tantrum as an example of how unfailingly genuine he is. "He's honest as hell," Ruth says. "He's brutally honest."

And shamelessly in pursuit of not just success, but

attention. Before an April, 1998, Timberwolves NBA basketball game against the Seattle Supersonics, Jesse rappelled down onto the court from the rafters to cheers from the fans. The local newspaper referred to him as the Timberwolves "unofficial mascot."

The Arbitron ratings of Jesse's show were skyrocketing—they quadrupled those of the syndicated sports shows KFAN had been running previously. Things were going great, both for Jesse and the station. His career was back on track.

Westerman kept hearing this nonsense about Jesse running for Governor. Jesse had flirted with a statewide run for Senate in '96, but had never followed through. But he seemed to be serious about this one.

"You know I'm running for Governor," he had told Westerman during their August 1997 contract negotiations.

"Yeah, yeah, yeah," Westerman said.

He thought to himself: *C'mon, Jesse, we have important things to talk about here.*

PART TWO

TEN

THE MAVERICK STATE

> *"[In both wrestling and politics] you travel a lot—especially to small towns, the Worthingtons, the Bird Islands. Wrestling is the only pro sport that goes to those places. We call them spot shows, and these are the spot shows of politics. It lets you get the message right out to the people."*[53]
>
> —JESSE VENTURA

Some states have electoral quirks that reflect the uniqueness of its populace. It's long been said that before a candidate can win a statewide race in Ohio, he needs to lose a statewide race at least once. Until recently, Texans hated to re-elect their governor, no matter how popular he or she may have been. And Minnesotans have a fiery populist streak—a love for bold ideas, straight talk, and political mavericks.

Residents of the twentieth most populous state—with 4,375,099 citizens, according to the 1990 census—still admire the political themes of straight-shooting and reform that led to the creation of the Farmer-Labor party that dominated state politics in the 1930s. The last vestiges of the Farmer-Labor party still exist in the state Democratic party, which is known as the Democratic-Farmer-Labor Party, or DFL.

Farmer-Labor Governor Floyd B. Olson, first elected in 1930, was known for supporting the lower-class, and made no bones about his gambling, skirt-chasing, or the dubious company he kept—which one author referred to as "a riffraff of Communists, Trotskyites, labor crooks, and other undesirables." Olson responded to questions about his questionable lifestyle by saying, presumably tongue-in-cheek, "That's a cross I got to bear, boys. Pray for me."

"I am not a liberal," Olson proclaimed another time, "I am what I want to be—a radical!"

Olson's shoot-from-the-hip style meshed perfectly with the odd and fanciful mindsets of Minnesota voters. "Minnesota is extremely volatile politically. It is a state pulled toward East and West both, and one always eager to turn the world upside down," one pundit wrote—in 1946.

Governor Harold Stassen was another example. The "Boy Governor," who served from 1939 until 1943, boldly decried the isolationist movements in his state. He later made a name for himself as a perennial presidential candidate—running for and losing the Republican nomination for President ten times between 1948 and 1992.

A candidate's party never seemed to be all that important to Minnesota voters—it was the man. "In the dynamics of Minnesota politics," observed another author, in 1970, "party lines have never seemed sacred."[54] And this was reflected in the state's strong tradition of remaining free from party labels. In 1944, a statewide poll indicated that "independents" held a plurality in the state's voter rolls—35%, compared with the DFL's 30% and the Republican Party's 32%.

Senator Hubert Humphrey was a proud product of the state. He first burst onto the national scene by demanding a civil rights plank in the Democrat Party's national platform in 1948. Twenty years later, however, Humphrey—then LBJ's vice president—was no longer a young firebrand, he was strictly status quo. And as a result of his continued support for the Vietnam War, Humphrey found himself fighting off a strong challenge for his party's Presidential nomination. The challenge was coming from a thoughtful young Senator who also hailed from Minnesota—Eugene McCarthy.

It was just that kind of state. Outspoken men of ambition and principle. A fickle electorate. Five out of the six presidential elections held from 1964 until 1984 included a Minnesotan on a major party ticket.

Twenty-two years after McCarthy's first Presidential run, another longshot statewide candidate emerged to challenge the status quo. He was an ex-wrestler with fiery rhetoric and close to no political experience. He was given almost no chance of winning. He ran political advertisements that were entertaining and wacky; the incumbent paid him little mind. By election day, however, the upstart had earned 50% of the vote; his opponent had garnered only 48%.

This victory, however, predated Jesse's by eight years. The stunning electoral success of Senator Paul Wellstone—a professor from liberal Carleton College and 1988 Minnesota co-chairman of Jesse Jackson for President—was just another example of the open-mindedness of the uncertain, no-bullshit voters from the land of 10,000 lakes.

Wellstone is one of the most liberal voices in the Senate, while Minnesota's other Senator, Rod Grams, is one of its most conservative. Voters here gave Ross Perot 24% of their vote in 1992; Perot received 12% of Minnesotans' Presidential vote in '96—three points higher than the national average. However homogenous its population might be—and 94% of the state is white—the ideas and trends floating around out there are hardly of whole cloth.

"I think part of it goes back to the Scandinavians who came here," says former Minnesota Governor and Senator Wendell Anderson. "There were strong cooperatives, and a history of political involvement."

Academics agree with former Governor Anderson's assessment, especially since the state boasts the highest percentage of Americans of Scandinavian origin than any other state—about one-third, by some counts. According to an essay in the 1977 volume *Perspectives on Minnesota: Government and Politics*, the roots of Minnesota's confounding electoral trends can be traced to the character of the Scandinavian people:

> "In Scandinavia, a tradition of democracy and political independence accompanied an antipathy toward the overstrict authority and bureaucracy ... protest was not long coming when the American dream went unfulfilled. Norwegians and Finns were particularly noted for participation and leadership in protest movements wherever they settled ... They rejected the party system also when it did not work well for them. Minnesota politicians found that they had to deliver on promises on the issues or Scandinavians would bolt to another party or start another interest group ... Scandinavians were the first to organize third parties which upset traditional issues-less politics."[55]

"They are way, way out in front of the elected officials," Anderson says. "The voters of Minnesota are sophisticated enough and mature enough that they can be told the truth.'' Anderson, for example, raised his state's taxes significantly—but he coupled the proposed tax hikes with a budget address and a trip around the state telling voters exactly what he was doing. ''In the next election out of eighty-seven counties, I won eighty-seven counties,'' he says.

But Anderson would ultimately feel the wrath of Minnesota voters as well. Two years later, in 1976, Senator Walter Mondale resigned to serve as President Jimmy Carter's vice president. Governor Anderson was given the opportunity to appoint someone as senator—he decided to appoint himself.

''It was a mistake,'' Anderson says today. ''At the time I thought I had the best chance to (politically) survive as a senator.'' But Minnesotans didn't like the hubris Anderson's self-appointment seemed to indicate and when he came up for re-election, they booted him from office. The weird and wildly unpredictable Minnesota voter had struck again.

It was in this arena that The Body found a crowd he could play to.

ELEVEN

DEAN BARKLEY

With such a voter base, it should come as no surprise that Minnesota has been on the forefront of various innovations in public policy. The state has served as the location of the country's first statewide educational choice plan and the nation's first anti-smoking bill. Minnesota was one of the first states to establish HMOs, attempt welfare reform, and pass a law protecting the employment rights of gays and lesbians.

"It's a state of mind," says Carleton College's Schier. "The Scandinavian tradition has favored good government on the basis of moral principle, and has supported the idea of taking risks in the name of experiment."

In the post-Watergate reform era, the Minnesota state government passed a number of laws to "open up the system . . . and allow all opinions to be heard," according to Schier. This manifested itself in some of the most progressive campaign legislation in the nation—both Election Day registration, which opened the voting process by allowing previously inactive voters to register and vote the same day, and public campaign financing.

Public campaign financing would ultimately give Jesse's campaign $330,000 in public funds it desperately needed. This was entirely former Reform Party

Senate candidate Dean Barkley, who had received more than 5% of the vote in his '94 and '96 campaigns—thus giving the Reform Party major party status.

If it hadn't been for Dean Barkley paving the way before him—at great personal sacrifice—there is no way Jesse would even have had a chance at winning.

Sue Barkley never thought of Dean as political when she first met him, back when she was in high school and he lived with her brother Tim at the University of Minnesota. She'd married another man right after graduation, and she and Dean had gone their separate ways. But then she'd divorced in '78, and there was Dean, sweet and genuine as he'd always been. They married in '82.

"I didn't even know he was interested in politics," Sue says. "I didn't even know it was a side he had. He kept it well hidden." For ten years of marriage, in fact. But in 1992, there was something about this thing that Ross Perot was doing. This wacky populist billionaire was speaking some sense, Dean thought.

Dean, an attorney and business consultant, found himself called to duty. Sue doesn't even remember how it all got started, exactly—one minute he was in the kitchen and some friend of his was telling him that he ought to run for office, and the next, he was running for the U.S. Congress as an Independent.

Sue was a Republican, and Dean had once worked for liberal Democrat George McGovern, but there was a third way to do it now, Dean said. "He thought he could make a difference," Sue says. Dean and she went out to collect the 2,000 signatures necessary to get him on the ballot. They went to the parking lot of

Rainbow's grocery store, they stood outside the government center at the library.

Friends chipped in. Five or six of the same people, they'd come over to the Barkley home and talk. "How are we going to raise money?" they asked. "How are we going to get money? How are we going to get his name out to the people?"

Dean and Sue took out a $30,000 second mortgage on their house. It wasn't enough. Election returns came in that November night, and Barkley had only earned 17% of the vote in his race for the congressional seat in Minnesota's sixth district. They were standing in the Medina Ball Room when returns came in. "We were disappointed," Sue says. "I wasn't sure if he'd run again." She sure didn't want him to.

But two years later, he decided to go for it again. Dean ran statewide this time, for U.S. Senate. He lost again, to former Representative Rod Grams, but Dean had secured more than 5% of the vote, meaning that the Reform Party had finally earned major party status in the state. That was his goal, anyway. In 1996, he ran again, against incumbent Senator Paul Wellstone. Again, he got more than 5%, a victory of sorts.

But where Dean thought he was piling up victories, his wife was demoralized. "He didn't work a lot," she says, since he was out campaigning so much, so she "had gone into sales . . . I was working straight commission." They were running out of money. "When your kids start asking you what color milk is," she says, that's when it got really difficult. "We're still paying off debt," she says.

"What are you doing this for?" she'd ask. "I'd really get upset about the bills we'd have, the mortgage we'd have—it drove me crazy. By the time the election returns came in, in 1996, it was, 'Don't ask me to ever run again.' "

"I think a lot of people thought that Dean was just a flake . . . At times *I* did," she says.

During his quixotic Senate run in '94, Dean had been a guest of a local radio host, Jesse Ventura, on his KSTP morning show. Jesse liked Dean and would have him on the air, mainly because nobody else took him seriously—Dean wasn't even allowed to participate in the debates. During his next race in '96, Dean named Jesse as his honorary campaign chairman. Jesse offered to march with Dean in a Fourth of July parade in Annandale, Dean's hometown. During the parade, though, it was the oddest thing—people were cheering Jesse on, not Dean.

"Jes-SEE! Jes-SEE! Jes-SEE!"

Dean turned to his large friend.

"The wrong guy is running here," Dean said. "Your turn is next."

"Dean, I don't want to go to Washington," Jesse replied. "I'll tell you what, though. I'll consider Governor, 'cause that keeps me in the state of Minnesota." He was half joking.

Barkley related the story to his campaign manager, Doug Friedline. Like the candidate whose campaign he was running, Friedline was a political junkie but far from an expert pol. A resident of Brooklyn Park, he made his living selling business forms and running a pulltab gambling operation in Ramsey.

After Friedline and Barkley's 1996 efforts came to their foregone, futile conclusion, the two men began discussing plans for '98. Arne Carlson, Minnesota's popular two-term governor, would be ending his reign, and plenty of prospective DFL and Republican candidates were publicly mulling over their chances of becoming the state's thirty-eighth governor. Friedline and Barkley wanted a Reform Party candidate in there somewhere, and were convinced that Jesse was the man for the job. They were trying to build a movement and start a political revolution, and though they had few delusions that the former pro wrestler could actually win, they had little doubt that he could pull in more votes than Dean did. Jesse would help put the party on the map.

They began lobbying Jesse to run, calling him a couple times a month. Ever since Jesse had been elected Mayor of Brooklyn Park, he'd imagined running for higher office. Senate, maybe. Governor, possibly. But it had all been talk. Now someone was proposing a run for real.

What else did he have going on? He enjoyed his work for KFAN, but that job would be there for him after the race was over. It was a new adventure, a new incarnation for the man with the franchise on re-creating himself.

He did have concerns. The timing was good for him—he was forty-six and looking for a new goal—but how about for Terry and the kids? Terry, then forty-two, was happy with the way things were. And though she was outgoing, she hated public life.

Then there were his kids. Ty had graduated and was talking about getting into the film industry. He'd become a fine young man, had turned out pretty great, in fact.

Jade, on the other hand, was more of a concern. Unfailingly sweet, she was different from Ty, more vulnerable. She received special education for her learning disability. Terry gave her a lot of attention and didn't want that to change. Jade was an amazing girl, they all thought, remarkable and boundlessly special. She had exceeded her doctor's hopes, had been riding horses since she was four and could play the piano and the flute. But she was just starting high school and Jesse valued her happiness and wanted to protect her as much as he could.

After several months of phone calls, in September, 1997, Jesse phoned up Barkley and told him to come out to the ranch. Barkley and Friedline drove out to Maple Grove.

Jesse asked Barkley what it would take, what it would be like to run statewide. They decided it would require about $400,000 to run credibly. They discussed the message they wanted to convey, the disenfranchised voters they wanted to reach. They were all amazed that a 50% voting rate was often considered a success in today's world. They wanted to reach those tens of thousands of voters who, like them, were turned off from politicians and politics in general. That's who they were going to go after, they decided. That's who they were going to inspire.

"Well," Jesse finally said. "I think I want to give it a try. But Dean—I'm the easy sell. Now we got to go out to the barn and convince Terry."

Jesse didn't make a move without talking with Terry. She usually backed his crazy schemes, but this one was different since it would unquestionably affect the children. They'd seen how poor Chelsea Clinton's life had changed after her parents moved into their new home in '92. That was the last thing either of them would want for Ty and Jade.

So Jesse, Dean, and Doug went out to the barn. They told Terry what they'd been talking about.

Terry told Dean that he'd have to clean the barn barefoot before she'd OK such a thing.

But then she and Jesse talked privately about the

race. Terry was adamant: She wanted the family kept out of it. She didn't want them exposed to public life. Jesse agreed. But he wanted to run.

"If I don't do it, who will?" he asked her. It could possibly be the end of the Reform Party in Minnesota if he didn't run, he said. She saw the fire in his eyes, knew how much he wanted to do this.

Eventually, she agreed. He could be pretty convincing when he wanted to be.

Later that fall, when "Mean" Gene Okerlund was in Minneapolis for a WCW event, Jesse hosted him on his KFAN show.

"Since you're no longer the mayor of that little podunk town, what are you gonna do next?" Okerlund recalls asking Jesse.

"Well, you know, Mean Gene—I might run for governor," Jesse replied.

"You're kidding," Okerlund said.

TWELVE

THE CANDIDATE

On January 26, 1998, Dean Barkley walked into Room 181 of the State House Building in St. Paul where reporters were waiting for him. For the first time, however, he wasn't there to announce his own candidacy—he was there to introduce Jesse Ventura as the Reform Party candidate for governor.

Reporters and political observers knew Barkley, and he had earned some measure of respect among them. "He's a smart guy," says political scientist Schier. "He has a long attention span, he knows the issues well, and he's very interested in the substance of politics. . . . He's quite the opposite of Jesse."

"Dean Barkley is the Moses" of Minnesota's Reform Party, says Schier. "Dean was willing to make himself a pauper in the pursuit of this political cause."

But the cause was no longer his. The doughy, sad-eyed Barkley stood in front of the press and said he was "passing the torch" to the former pro wrestler. He noted that Jesse had both higher name recognition and more government experience than then-Senator Rod Grams, who had been a Twin Cities anchorman before he ran for the House in 1992. He referred to Jesse as a "rational, common-sense centrist."

And then Barkley stepped aside.

From the very beginning of his candidacy, it was

clear that Jesse's strength was also his weakness: he was Jesse Ventura, outspoken, constantly shooting from the hip.

Still, he did modify his look somewhat for the race. As he continually re-invented himself, mutating his original wrestling persona to serve as announcer, actor, mayor, and radio talk show host, Jesse also was no stranger to changing around his look. As a pro wrestler, he went in and out of various style and fashions— not to mention the constantly changing facial hair topography. Now Jesse was preparing for political life, so a thing or two had to be adjusted.

One day on his KFAN talk show, Jesse was rapping on the phone with Gene Deckerhoff—his former colleague from his days with the Buccaneers.

"Mean Gene, I'm running for governor," he told him.

"Jesse, let me ask you: last time I saw you, you had a chrome dome and a little piggy tail, you still look like that?" Deckerhoff asked.

"Mean Gene, I still got the dome, but I shaved off the piggytail," Jesse said. "I shaved off that rascal to run for office."

As he spoke with the political reporters that day in St. Paul, Jesse was charming and glib. He joked with them about having to re-shoot a scene in *Batman and Robin* where Uma Thurman kissed him. He said he was running because he wanted "to find out if the American dream is dead. I want to find out if you have to be a career politician to lead and govern the state."

His campaign stump speech—from that day until the last day of the election—focused on two items: taxes and a government made up of career politicians. He was against both.

"I will veto any raising of taxes over the next four

years," he said. The state had recently showed a $4 billion budget surplus; Jesse was enraged that that money had been spent instead of returned to the taxpayers. "I had no intention of running for office until that $4 billion surplus showed up,"[56] he would later say.

As part of his effort to distinguish himself from the other politicians in the race, Jesse pledged that he would accept no PAC money, nor any individual contribution larger than $50. "Don't judge a candidacy by how much money they raise," he said. "That puts a candidate in debt. That means the candidate owes somebody." (Jesse knew the dance of quid pro quo firsthand, of course, from his successful experience lobbying Congress to secure funding for Highway 610. Though not surprisingly, he didn't mention this.)

Reporters asked him questions about policy and law, issues that a gubernatorial candidate ought to know about. Jesse acknowledged that he had some things to learn. He was candid about his ignorance. He was coming to the people with a general concept of how he felt the state ought to be run—specifics would follow. He went into his mayoral experience the same way, and that turned out all right in the end. "There are people who thought Brooklyn Park was going to dry up and die when I won. It didn't," he reminded the media.

Most of the performance was funny and charming and utterly insignificant, reporters thought. Jesse was quick with the one-liners—"Elections and politics are pretty much like war without guns, and I'm pretty good at it," he said—but surely he hadn't a snowball's chance in hell.

No third-party candidate had won a statewide election in more than half a century, political reporters said to one another. And this guy? *Please.* When he was asked what made him qualified to be governor, he cited his experiences as a Navy SEAL twenty-five years before. When asked to sum up his campaign, he said, ''Let's put Minnesotans first. There's more of us than there are Democrats and Republicans.'' Surely this guy would be good for some good copy, but that was about it. After all, there were some major players running for governor that year.

THIRTEEN

MY THREE SONS

As election season unofficially began at the start of 1998, reporters from the *New York Times* and the *Washington Post* converged on Minnesota for the great story of the governor's race—but Jesse wasn't even necessarily mentioned in these articles. The great story that the political reporters were flying in to cover was the oddity of the DFL primary—which pitted the *sons* of many of Minnesota's former greats against one another.

First and foremost there was Hubert "Skip" Humphrey III, fifty-five, the state's attorney general for fourteen years. Humphrey, son of the former vice president, was well-known to many voters due to the highly publicized public fights he'd waged against deadbeat dads, teen pregnancy, crime, and, most recently, tobacco companies.

Humphrey's biggest rival for the DFL endorsement was Minneapolis' Mike Freeman, forty-nine, the Hennepin County Attorney. Freeman was the son of former Minnesota Governor Orville Freeman, who'd served alongside Skip's dad in the Johnson Administration as secretary of agriculture.

There was also forty-year-old Ted Mondale, son of former Vice President Walter Mondale, who'd served in the state Senate for six years. Unlike Humphrey and

Freeman, Mondale had been staking out centrist "New Democrat" positions.

There were other candidates, of course—the richest of whom was Mark Dayton, fifty-one, heir to the Midwest department store chain of the same name. But to reporters who came from the East coast to write a "My Three Sons" profile of the DFL primary, Skip, Mike, and Ted were the story. One of the three, the stories noted, would end up facing off against Republican St. Paul Mayor Norm Coleman, a savvy former Humphrey staffer who'd switched parties only a year before.

"A state that loves politics," summed up the *Washington Post*'s David Broder. "[A]n intriguing governor's race is taking place here . . . It's a great cast of characters," he wrote, before summarizing the Three Sons, as well as Coleman and his opponents. And then, as an afterthought, Broder wrote, "And if that were not enough, there's Reform Party candidate Jesse Ventura, a shaven-head former pro wrestler."

One of the very many reasons pundits discounted Jesse was his refusal to accept PAC money. In politics, money doesn't just talk, it screams and yells and stomps around the room. Candidates need money to print up lawn signs and posters, pay their staffs, travel around the state or district, fund polling and Get-Out-the-Vote telephone banks, and—most importantly—pay for television and radio advertisements.

A gubernatorial candidate could spend every day of election season at malls and shopping centers, meeting voters and charming the pants off them, but in the end he wouldn't make even a dent come election night if he or she hadn't appeared on TV. Candidacies aren't taken very seriously—by reporters and voters alike—if they lack the means for serious advertising.

By limiting the donations coming into his campaign, Jesse was taking a bold step, a symbolic step, and—insiders thought—a foolish one. Since Barkley had secured major party status for Jesse, he would have some public financing cash flowing his way—but only if Jesse stood at 5% in the polls himself close to election day.

Money quickly started pouring into the race. By early February—before election season had even really begun—more than a million dollars had already been raised by the DFL candidates. Dayton had raised $405,740; Mondale had $365,717; Humphrey had $261,353; and Freeman had $237,183.

Coleman, who was facing minor opposition for the Republican nomination, had raised $112,767.

And Jesse had raised $1,195. And of that paltry sum, only $244 was actually available.

Jesse did have one factor working for him: name recognition. Voters had heard of him. A February *Star Tribune*/KMSP-TV poll showed that Jesse enjoyed 64% name recognition in the state. Of course, Humphrey (89%), Mondale (70%), and Coleman (76%) were all ranked higher.

FOURTEEN

140 MPH

Jesse ran his race the only way he knew how: he was bluntly, honestly, brutally himself.

One reporter asked him how fast his Porsche could go.

"You know that high stretch of road leaving town out of Two Harbors?" he replied. "I've had it up to 140 there."[57]

He was as direct with questions about policy, winning converts slowly but surely as he offered straightforward answers to questions about, say, the state's tax surplus (Give it back! he said). In interviews and on the stump, pressing the flesh or on KFAN, he offered voters straight, non-focus-group-tested, unresearched common sense. It was the way common folk talked when they talked politics. There was none of that "At this point in time" or "Not to the best of my recollection" horseshit. When people—real *people,* not the automotons on C-SPAN—talked politics, they talked like Jesse did.

Jesse's frankness was particularly refreshing in 1998, a year that political prevarication besmirched the highest political office in the land indefinitely when President Clinton denied and denied and denied having a sexual relationship with a young White House intern named Monica Lewinsky. Beginning at the end of January, President Clinton began issuing statements to the press and prosecutors that took the art of diction to new levels.

"There is *no* relationship," he would say to one reporter in February—factually true since the relationship had been in the past. "I did not have sexual relations with that woman," he would indignantly lecture the American people—true in his mind, at least, since he defined "sexual relations" as intercourse. Clinton would even later defend his wordsmithing by smugly explaining that the truthfulness of one of his grand jury statements depended upon "what your definition of 'is' is."

As the political battle of President Clinton's life dragged on, and Washington, D.C., sank into a miasma of legalistic hair-splitting, spin and counterspin, a voice like Jesse's was indeed a *vox clamantis in deserto*. Under these special circumstances, his candor, simple declarations of general principle, and even his occasional naïveté played well.

Especially with disenfranchised voters. As soon as she heard on the radio that Jesse might run, Mavis Huddle—a sixty-four-year-old retired secretary from Brooklyn Park who walked with a cane—called Jesse up and volunteered, becoming Jesse's secretary, scheduler, and advance woman.

Friedline, the only paid staffer, worked with Jesse and Barkley to build a rag-tag campaign staff. In February, Phil Madsen, an unmarried forty-four-year-old computer consultant and former founder of Minnesota's Independence Party, volunteered to build a Website for the campaign. Though he'd never designed a Website before, Madsen set to the task, buying a copy of Microsoft FrontPage 98 and finding a Website host that only charged $30 a month.

Barkley also brought aboard his former campaign press secretary, Gerry Drewery, a sixty-eight-year-old semi-retired public relations consultant who also worked part time as a reporter for the *Farmington Independent*.

As Jesse's senior advisors put together his campaign staff, Jesse insisted that his campaign would mimic the uniqueness of the candidate.

"I have one rule, and one rule only," he told his staff. "This is going to be fun. The moment we stop having fun will be the moment I withdraw from the race." His campaign had a simple, declarative theme that summed it all up: Retaliate in '98.

In May, Jesse made one last attempt to work in films, hedging his bets on his gubernatorial bid by acting in *20/20 Vision,* an independent film written and directed by twenty-four-year-old Christopher Newberry.

The twenty-minute, $25,000 dark comedy, eventually rejected by the Sundance Film Festival, tells the story of a young couple sucked into the underworld of marriage counseling. Jesse plays Buddy "One Arm" Sanchez, a disturbed marriage counselor who serves as the centerpiece of the film. At the end of *20/20 Vision,* Buddy "One Arm" Sanchez goes nuts and turns violent.

"Sanchez is a villain, and he has to do some morally compromising things," Newberry says. "If the footage had gotten out, it could have been seen in the wrong light, and someone could have gotten the wrong impression."

"This isn't going to be showing anywhere in the next few months, is it?" Jesse asked.

The same month, Attorney General Skip Humphrey was tending to his professional projects as well. Minnesota and Blue Cross/Blue Shield of Minnesota settled their lawsuit against the tobacco industry to the tune of $6.1 billion.

In downtown Minneapolis, reporters and editors at the political desk of the state's leading newspaper— the Minneapolis *Star Tribune*, nicknamed the *Strib*— didn't even think Jesse's candidacy merited the time and effort of a full-time political reporter. In the spring, they met to decide who would cover each candidate. Jesse was assigned to Bob von Sternberg, a forty-six-year-old general assignment scribe who'd been with the *Strib* since '85.

"At that point, it looked like three or four stories and maybe a day on the campaign trail with him," von Sternberg says. "The paper generally doesn't do much with minor party candidates."

The *Scrib*, as well as the rest of the state's press corps, were busy covering the behind-the-scenes machinations of the Republican party, as well as the brutally competitive horserace for the DFL nomination. Humphrey was the highly favored contender; a poll released in early June showed that, if the primary vote had been held then—as opposed to September 15—he would receive 38% of the vote, a plurality victory. Freeman garnered less than half that, tying with Dayton for a far far second place score of 15%.

But DFL voters were not represented well by their DFL delegates, who favored Freeman. This was typical in Minnesota; the state's political parties had long been falling captive to the extremes of each party. In June, at the National Hockey Center at St. Cloud State University, after a highly contested few months of battle, and on the tenth ballot, Freeman actually beat Humphrey for the DFL endorsement. To everyone watching, it just showed how clueless and anachronistic the DFL party had grown.

A few weeks later, Coleman secured the GOP endorsement in his party's least divisive convention in years.

The DFL candidates had spent the summer barreling for each other in attempts to win the party endorsement in June and the nomination in September. They participated in maybe three million debates. Meanwhile, Coleman fended off challenges from the religious right and shored up his conservative credentials to placate the doubters who questioned his recent conversion to their party. No one paid much attention to the pro wrestler.

When he wasn't at KFAN, Jesse hit the campaign trail, shaking hands, granting media interviews, answering questions about various issues. Though he generally refrained from getting bogged down in the intricate details of the tax code or farming policy, he started to take sides.

Jason Lewis, Jesse's former colleague at KSTP, started to take Jesse to task for some of his positions. *How could Jesse oppose public financing for a new Twins ballpark when he supported it to build the Target Center, where the NBA's Timberwolves played?* Lewis asked. It couldn't be as simple as the fact that Jesse was an ardent Timberwolves fan, while he wasn't that much into baseball, could it? Lewis, a staunch Republican who supported Coleman, was one of the few members of the media challenging Jesse's opinions, and treating him like an actual, credible, candidate.

That wasn't how Jesse saw it, however. Jesse started to seethe. Who was Lewis to berate him? Politicians need to have thick skins—once you enter public life, the slings and arrows start coming from every direction, for reasons both valid and irresponsible. But this wasn't Jesse—he fought back, he got angry, he got even.

On Saturday, June 7, the Reform Party held its convention at Jesse's alma mater, North Hennepin Community College. The convention was all too similar to those of the other parties, and that Saturday it got bogged down in the minutia of politics—something about negotiations on bylaws or some such nonsense.

Jesse was getting anxious. Terry's family was getting together near Mankato that night—he needed to be there. Could they hurry it up? He grew restless. He told a few people that he couldn't wait much longer.

When the delegates heard that their star was about to take off, they suspended debate. Barkley nominated him, and Russ Verney, the chairman of the national Reform Party, introduced the party's nominee for governor.

Jesse strode to the stage—the first time he'd been on that podium since he was in Aristophanes' *The Birds*, way back in the seventies. Things had changed a bit in some ways. And in other, more personal, ways, they hadn't changed at all.

He looked out at the 109 convention delegates, who'd unanimously endorsed him.

He rallied his troops. Don't worry about the polls, he said. Polls are bullshit. More importantly, Humphrey and Coleman—the two likely nominees—their polls numbers were at their highest. Their numbers were only going to sink, Jesse said. No one even knew Jesse was in the game and running for the endzone, so they would ignore him and his approval ratings were only going to rise.

"We're gonna lay in the weeds like good Navy

SEALs,'' Jesse told the crowd. ''and when they are two other candidates left standing, we're gonna swoop in!''[58]

The crowd went wild; they ate it up. Again, he held an audience in the palm of his hand, and he loved it.

As the Reform Party aspired to act like a real party, forming a platform and running a convention, Jesse made attempts to act like a legitimate candidate. While carving out a markedly different niche, Jesse still had to do and say certain things in order to be taken seriously—filling out candidate questionnaires, forming opinions on subjects he neither knew nor cared about, and, of course, picking a nominee for lieutenant governor.

Dean had been his first choice. But Dean said he had to check with Sue, his wife, and Sue's response was succinct: ''Not if you want me to be your wife,'' she said, and that was the end of that discussion. Dean became Jesse's campaign chair instead.

Then Jesse went to former Minnesota Twin first baseman Kent Hrbek. But Hrbek didn't want to spend his year pressing palms—it would clearly interfere with his fishing, hunting, and bowling.

In February, the *Strib* had published a poll showing that education weighed heavily on the minds of voters. Jesse, Dean, and Doug had seen that poll, and were heavily influenced by it. They had originally thought of making crime more of an issue—Jesse was so proud of the crime stats in Brooklyn Park, after all—but they decided to emphasize education instead. The poll also led Jesse and his campaign to another refreshing, bold, and somewhat naive decision. How do you show people that you care about education? Put a schoolteacher on the ticket, of course.

Sixty-four-year-old Mae Schunk didn't remember

Jesse from his wrestling days—she thought she remembered him as a Good Guy—but she knew about Jesse "The Candidate" Ventura, alright. A mutual friend recommended Schunk to Jesse and they sat down to talk. Schunk had grown up on a dairy farm in Wisconsin, and had been teaching for thirty-six years, twenty-two of them in the St. Paul school system. Her expertise was in working with gifted children, though she'd also developed school curricula and had been an assistant principal. She lived in Grove Heights with her husband Bill, and had one adult son.

Jesse liked her. And appointing Schunk—like Jesse, a real person, one who had never run for major office before—seemed to be the way to properly focus on education, an area Jesse knew little-to-nothing about. He'd hand off the whole matter to her, let a teacher run things for a while. And why not? Her first priority would be to concentrate on improving the state's teacher-to-student ratio.

On June 30, Jesse held a press conference to introduce Schunk as his running mate.

Taxes were the number one issue for his campaign, Jesse said, but "education is my second major concern. I am a product of the Minneapolis public schools, and I am a supporter of the public schools. But I do not pretend to have the answers to all of the problems in schools today. So I have turned to an expert . . ."

As the campaign plodded on through the summer, Jesse frequently joined the DFL candidates in debates, while Coleman kept away. Next to polished pols Humphrey, Freeman, Mondale, and the others, Jesse seemed like another species altogether.

The two-hour candidate forum of July 1, for instance, would have been unbearable were Jesse not there. As the pols gave the same pat answers, the same non-controversial faux-boldness, the man who played Abraxas, Guardian of the Universe seemed to be the only man up on stage who was of this earth.

When it was his turn to answer a question about illiterate kids graduating from school, Jesse bragged on Schunk, of course, but then said something almost heretical. "It doesn't come to the teacher being Number One, it comes to parents being Number One," Jesse said. "When you hear about kids falling through the cracks—excuse me, if you're a parent who pays attention, don't you realize in third grade when little Johnny comes home and can't read or write that something's missing here? It comes back to you as parents. Parents have to take an active role. You can't shift the burden to the teachers; you can't shift it to government."

Jesse's gruff—but charming—ways often surprised people who were hearing him for the first time. He was like Ronald Reagan in that regard. Knowing little about the man except for his most basic bio, people expected an idiot. They found in his place a regular guy with a truckload of integrity, a modicum of wit, and some thought-out answers to many of their questions.

The *Politics in Minnesota* newsletter noted that, "People who see [Jesse] for the first time are pleasantly surprised. They expect a knuckle-dragger with a monosyllabic vocabulary. Instead, they get a guy who seems to understand what he's saying and can periodically be funny and charming when he says it."

Still, it wasn't enough. Not yet, anyway.

And then, suddenly, Jesse had a competitor for the Reform Party nomination. Barkley was pissed. Who was this guy, this "Bill Dahn," anyway?

The forty-eight-year-old Dahn seemed something of

a crank—he said he was running to reveal some sort of "corruption" and he alluded to some sort of cover-up. Some even thought Dahn dangerous. Mayor Coleman had filed a complaint against Dahn with the police, alleging that Dahn had made threats against him—having phoned his office almost 100 times in just over a year. Dahn had been placed under a restraining order in June 1996.

Regardless, Dahn had paid the $300 filing fee and was all set to face off against Jesse for the nomination.

Jesse didn't want an opponent for any number of reasons, but foremost among them was the fact that KFAN management had been talking about taking him off the air ever since this governor thing had become a reality. Management was worried that if they allowed Jesse to continue with his radio show they'd be accused of giving him an unfair advantage over the other candidates. There were FCC regulations to worry about, a station to run—issues far more important that one employee's quixotic campaign.

Jesse was trying to convince his bosses to let him stay on the air at least until September 15, the date of the primary. He loved his job, enjoyed the forum, but most of all he had a family to support and KFAN was his primary source of income. And here was this loose cannon, Dahn, who no one ever heard of. Dahn's presence on the Reform Party ballot ruined Jesse's argument that there was no real race until September 15.

Dean took care of the problem. He had a talk with Dahn, convinced him to run against Coleman for the GOP spot. Dean even paid the $600 filing fee necessary for Dahn to switch parties. Problem solved.

Except it wasn't, really. Because KFAN management was serious about making Jesse take the leave of absence.

"We want to make sure that when you win, nobody can say that you were on the air too long," they said, according to Ruth, Jesse's producer. "At first, Jesse was like, 'Awwww, come on, guys.'"

But management held firm. Tuesday, July 21, the day that Jesse formally filed as a candidate, was his last day on KFAN.

Jesse was angry. It wasn't fair—Humphrey could go on as Attorney General, Coleman as Mayor of St. Paul, both of them cashing government checks as they had all their lives, while *they* ran for governor. Why couldn't *he* stay at his job in the private sector?! His family had to eat, too!

"It's my job," he would say. "I have to earn a living like everyone else . . . I'm not like the politicians. Why don't they have to take an unpaid leave of absence?!"

"Talk to The Bod while you still can," he told his listeners on his last day. "They sit at the right hand of God—Father, Son, and the FCC."

"The station just did what they felt they legally had to do," Ruth says.

Jesse left KFAN. But before he did so, he and Westerman made plans for his triumphant return on Wednesday, November 4—the day after he was to have lost the election.

Barkley was sure of it—*something* was going on out there, the electorate was taking Jesse seriously, even if the press and the politicians weren't. As Jesse worked his booth at the Minnesota State Fair that August, it was impossible not to look and wonder just what was afoot. The people crowded in to see Jesse, buying "Retaliate in '98" T-shirts—more than $26,000 worth. They told him they were going to vote for him. They took almost 50,000 Ventura/Schunk brochures.

Was it just because Jesse was a semi-celebrity, having worked Minnesota State Fair booths before for KFAN and others? Was it because Minnesotans were so disgusted with what was going on in Washington, D.C.?

Hubert "Buck" Humphrey IV, Skip's son, is convinced that Zippergate pushed a few voters to Jesse. "In back of peoples' mind was this whole impeachment process," Buck says. "Another disconnect between Washington and Minnesota."

Polls indicated that Jesse's support was growing, too. One poll from early June had Jesse registering as the gubernatorial choice of 7% of the voters. That support had doubled by September 1, as Jesse garnered 13%, Humphrey held steady with 43%, and Coleman with 29%.

Whatever "it" was—whether Ventura/Schunk were tapping into a reservoir of good will, or resentment, or some mixture of the two—it wasn't manifesting itself in any cash for the Reform party candidates. By the end of August, Coleman had raised more than Humphrey and Mondale combined. The St. Paul Mayor had put $1.4 million in his campaign coffers. Skip Humphrey had put $671,345 in the bank; with the help of donations from Hollywood as well as his dad's former boss, Jimmy Carter, Ted Mondale had a net of $635,088.

Jesse had raised $61,121.

Many lawyers and lobbyists were hedging their bets, of course, donating to both Skip *and* Coleman. Many even chipped in to some of Skip's DFL rivals. These influence-peddlers contributed $660,000 to just six of the candidates. Of that, Jesse got not even one penny.

Surprising no one, Skip Humphrey won the DFL nomination victory on September 15 with 37% of the vote. Coleman fared even better in his primary, garnering 91% to Dahn's 9%. Now it was a race.

Among the blabbocracy, Jesse's candidacy had risen to the level of "spoiler" status. Pundits viewed him as a candidate who would no doubt influence the race—but only because his 13% (or whatever) would amount to votes that could otherwise have helped either of his opponents.

Though Jesse had won 100% of the Reform Party vote, that only amounted to 16,297 votes—with only 9% of the GOP vote, after all, even Dahn had gotten 12,191 people to vote for *him*.

Over at the *Strib*, von Sternberg sat down with the paper's political writers and editors to talk about how they were going to cover Jesse.

"OK, what if he *does* win?" one of them asked. No one thought it would happen, but it was the tack they would have to take. Plus, at least, he made good copy.

FIFTEEN

AND THEN THERE WERE THREE

Raised in a garden of privilege and fame, and largely in Washington, D.C., Skip Humphrey got his dad's smarts but inherited little of his shine.

"The *idea* of Skip Humphrey is more impressive than Skip Humphrey," says political science professor Schier. "You hear about this crusading attorney general, who's won a record-setting tobacco deal and run a great office—fighting for consumer protection.... He's a real pioneer. And then you meet him. And you walk away and think 'This is him?' "

Skip stood before voters like a junior high school principal subbing for an absent teacher—he was someone the students didn't really know, though they knew of him; he was a man with a position of power over them; a man who thought he knew what was good for them ... whether it would reveal itself in a lesson, threat, or leadership was anyone's guess.

As Skip stumped around the state, he was gloomy, talking about Minnesota as if it were New York City's Bowery at the end of the nineteenth century. So many kids were without health insurance, *this* was falling apart, *that* was a tragedy of epic proportions. But life in Minnesota was good, generally, with crime down and a fat budget surplus and unemployment hovering around 2%. No one questioned Skip's sincerity, his desire to improve life, but this wasn't his father's world of 1948, nor even 1968, and his shrill bullet points came across as whining.

You kind of felt sorry for the guy—he was smart and well-meaning, surely he deserved some recognition for all the good that he'd done. But he conjured forth the image of a large, lumpy plate of oatmeal.

"Skip is not a great debater," says a Humphrey advisor. "The Humphrey genes don't want to let him say anything in less than thirty seconds . . . So those formats are just lousy for him."

"The more people saw of Skip," Schier says, "the less they were impressed by him."

Norm Coleman was another creature altogether. A tough Jewish kid from Brooklyn, NY, Coleman had been a Vietnam war protester at Long Island's Hofstra University. He traveled the country as a roadie for the band Ten Years After. "Then he dries out . . . and . . . goes to Iowa Law School," says Schier.

In '83, Coleman started working for none other than Attorney General Skip Humphrey. They became friends. In '88, Coleman cut his teeth in campaign politics by working on Humphrey's losing Senate bid.

He thought he'd make a pretty good candidate himself, so after ten years under Skip's tutelage, Coleman went out on his own, running as a Democrat for Mayor of St. Paul, the second largest city in the state. Humphrey even endorsed him despite the fact that the DFL had thrown their support behind someone else. In '96, right before his re-election bid, Coleman changed parties, becoming a Republican—and a conservative one at that, opposing legal abortions as well as gay rights.

"The problem with Coleman is who the hell *is* this guy?" Schier says. "Is he a campus radical? A conservative Republican? Or is he just trying on these different hats?'' Though Coleman was smart and even somewhat charismatic, there was something vaguely slippery about the guy.

After a post-primary *Strib* poll placed Humphrey twenty points ahead of his Republican rival, 49% to 29%, Humphrey was immediately labeled the man to beat. A Humphrey advisor says that Skip and his campaign knew that the *Strib* poll was way off. ''Our internal numbers showed that it was anything from a dead heat to a single-digit lead, but nothing like what the poll had us, at twenty points up,'' he reports.

The tenor of the campaign got ugly fast. ''I had to start denting Skip because he was way ahead,'' Coleman says. ''I had to challenge that.''

After Humphrey backed out of a Minnesota Chamber of Commerce debate, the state GOP hired a guy to follow him around, dressed like a chicken, accusing the attorney general of ''chickening out'' of debating Coleman. (This was an interesting charge for Coleman to make, since he had been invited to the seventeen billion pre-primary DFL debates and had refrained from attending any of them.)

On the very day of the primary, in fact, the state GOP had unveiled a TV ad which damned Humphrey for voting, in 1973, ''to decriminalize drugs and reduce the minimum sentence for murder to fifteen years. What's more,'' the woman's voice narrated, ''he even voted to make first-degree murderers eligible for parole . . .'' (Again, drug legalization was an interesting subject for Coleman—a former pot-smoking student protester and roadie—to raise.)

Humphrey decided to retaliate. Feeding perceptions that there was maybe a bit of instability behind Coleman's blow-dried veneer, Humphrey said that his former protégé was "risky" and "untested." A Humphrey TV ad plastered the words "false" and "slippery" next to Coleman's face.

"Norm could sell ice to the Eskimos," says a Humphrey advisor. "And his chameleon-like politics certainly plays a role in the slickness. That's why when we called him slick or various adjectives to tarnish him or paint him with that image, it started to stick. . . . Because there was a great element of truth to it."

Though such negativity is commonplace in the modern-day campaign, when the bell rang and the hits started coming in fast and furious for this race, it was still only September—an extremely early moment in their meet for the fighting to get so ugly. And there was a third, increasingly credible, candidate who wasn't getting bruised up.

Conventional wisdom continued to hold that Jesse's candidacy would suck votes away from Coleman. "Humphrey will win because Jesse Ventura, like Coleman a deep tax-cutter, will take too many votes from the St. Paul mayor," wrote the St. Paul *Pioneer Press* business editor. "Ventura's Reform message, anti-tax and anti-big government, is more compatible with Republican philosophy," opined the publisher and co-editor of the *Politics in Minnesota* newsletter in a *Strib* op-ed.

At the September 18 Governor's Economic Summit, Humphrey was a no-show, purportedly protesting the fact that Jesse hadn't been invited to speak. (He'd actually been in California raising money, but didn't want to publicize that fact.) Prompted by a phone call from Friedline, state senate majority leader Roger Moe—Humphrey's running mate for the LG spot—ceded half of his time to Jesse, who strode to the podium in black Levi's, a camouflage shirt, an Australian bushman's hat not unlike that of Blain in *Predator*.

"You're going to find me a little bit different," Jesse said. With Humphrey's (or, rather, Moe's) insistence that Jesse be included in the September 18 forum, it has become Minnesota lore that Humphrey shot himself in the foot by announcing that he wouldn't appear at any of the gubernatorial debates unless Jesse, too, was invited. This wasn't quite what happened. "At the time people, called it a brilliant move," says the Humphrey advisor, "and in hindsight they call it a blunder. But it wasn't either one. The truth is that, according to the League of Women Voters, Jesse had already been invited to all the debates except for that first one, which was more like a forum."

It is true, however, that Skip and his campaign "believed his message—libertarian and fiscally conservative—would draw more Republicans than it did Democrats," according to a source in the Humphrey campaign. The Coleman campaign's polling showed an altogether different phenomenon. "As Jesse's poll numbers were coming up, it was clear that Jesse was taking from Skip's voters, too," Coleman recalls.

On October 1, at the first gubernatorial debate at Central Lakes College in Brainerd, Humphrey and Coleman went at each other like steroid-fed roosters in a cockfight.

Humphrey will tax you into submission, Coleman said. Humphrey fired back with some nonsense about "Colemanomics." The two men had a history, and in the acid spewn from their tongues, you could see that it wasn't just all part of the job. It was personal.

It got particularly rough after a question about family farms. Coleman was pissed. Humphrey had been trying to portray him as an out-of-touch urbanite, misrepresenting his position on family farms in a TV com-

mercial. Coleman started ticking off bullet points as
to how his family farm platform differed from Skip's:
moratoriums on livestock, workers comp reform, Eth-
anol, bladdy bladdy blah.

"We have records," Coleman said. "As I've said,
I've cut taxes . . . I'll deliver on that; Skip has a record
of spending, he's gonna deliver on that. But the fact
is, Skip, you *didn't* quote what was in the paper. You
got up there on TV and said, 'I heard Norm Coleman
say . . . ' and you *didn't* hear me say. The fact is, if
we're gonna do this let's be fair, let's be straightforward, let's be honest, lets look at the record, let's fight
about our different views on the family farm."

Humphrey was asked to respond. He looked like a
big sour lump. His hands were folded in his lap and
his legs shifted uncomfortably.

"I just merely say," Skip retorted, "that I have
quoted exactly what is in the paper. But the reality
here, its not about what we say, it's what are we gonna
do for family farmers, that's the bottom line. And
frankly, Norm, if you don't understand what the family farm's all about, you oughta admit it, and go find
out about it. I can tell you this, they're not cash-
flowing *anything* today, they're going down the tubes.
And we need to make those kind of changes—"

"And Skip—" Coleman interrupted.

"—and the—" Skip continued.

"—and Skip, they don't want moratoriums—"
Coleman said.

"—changes in government ought to be involved
directly in that effort—" said Skip.

They were now both speaking at same time, creating an indecipherable cacophony of political pollu-
tion.

"—they want fair and free trade, which you oppose, they don't want moratoriums on livestock, and *they don't want you to roll back workers comp reform*—''

''—they want fair trade—''

''—I'm for free trade—''

The moderator finally interrupted and said it was time to let Jesse weigh in. Wearing a sports jacket over a golf shirt, and sneakers—he was about to go coach the Champlin Park High School football game—Jesse had a shining opportunity. And he took it.

''Well, I figure this shows, obviously, who's above all of this,'' Jesse said, standing in freshly starched whites next to two soiled mud wrestlers.

The room erupted with laughter. But Jesse had a point to make.

''I think right now, if you want to look at fair and good campaigning, I will just state this, that I'm embarrassed as a United Stated citizen and as a veteran to what both of these two premier parties—the Democrats and the Republicans—are sinking to today, from Washington to right on down here locally. I noticed a cartoon the other day in the *Star Tribune* newspaper where it kind of took a shot and said, 'Amazing, the only candidate that's campaigning on the issues and not slinging mud is the former pro wrestler, actor, and talk show host.' ''

''Jesse was pretty masterful there, because the reality is that he took his shots, too,'' says a source in the Humphrey campaign. ''But he had the humor and the timing to make it look like he was the guy who was staying above the fray. While, in fact, he was engaging in the fray, he was just doing it in a much more entertaining manner by his style, so he got away with it.''

A lot of Jesse's answers in the first debate—as

throughout his campaign—were simplistic. "If it's good for Minnesota, I'll sign it," he said, "if it's bad for Minnesota, I'll veto it."

The simple tune provided a melody of peace and the possibility of a new way, rising above the din of negativism and the tiresomeness of intricate detail that his two opponents constantly fed. "Jesse ran with an attitude, not with an agenda," says a Humphrey advisor. Which may not be a criticism. He was *different*, that was for sure. He didn't take PAC money, for one, a topic he raised at almost every possible juncture.

And, though he'd pledged to veto any proposed tax increases and return the state's budget surplus, Jesse also—unlike a politician—refused to promise no new taxes, a promise George Bush had made in 1988, and broken a few years later. "I'm a realist," Jesse said, "and I'm not going to make any false statements to get elected, because to me making budgets on expected surpluses—well, if that expected surplus doesn't show up, then both of these budgets mean nothing and they're just simply being used in an attempt to get elected."

True enough, though unfair in a way, since Jesse certainly was also using his anti-tax stance as mortar in his road to the Governor's Mansion. Pledging to veto tax increases while refusing to make a No New Taxes ultimatum was, characteristically, Jesse having it both ways. But it didn't seem to matter. It sounded good. And new.

In other ways in that first debate, Jesse defined himself. Accompanying his fiscal conservatism was an extremely liberal social mindset. In 1997, the Minnesota legislature had passed a "Defense of Marriage" Act, banning the state from recognizing gay and lesbian marriages that occurred in other states. Coleman trumpeted the bill. (His campaign had, in fact, prepared a negative TV ad blasting Humphrey for his stance against the act, though it pulled the ad from the airwaves in the immediate wake of the brutal murder of a gay University of Wyoming student, Matthew Shepard.)

That Humphrey would oppose the act seemed predictable, but when Jesse's turn to answer the question arose, he surprised more than a few members of the voting public by relating a touching personal view of gay rights. "I have two friends that have been together forty-one years," he said. "If one of them becomes sick, the other one is not even allowed to be at the bedside. I don't believe government should be so hostile, so mean-spirited . . . Love is bigger than government."

The *Brainerd Dispatch* had no problem sorting out the results of the first debate. "Ventura Wins Audience's Decision," was their headline the next day. " 'He was the only one actually answering all of the questions,' " one resident of Pequot Lakes said. "The other guys seemed to mumble on quite a bit. Jesse was the only one who seemed to hit the issues that needed hitting," said a local high school senior.

"The guy is a very effective communicator," a Humphrey advisor says. "Take how he sold himself as the common man. . . . The thing about it is Jesse Ventura is a guy who lives in a ranch mansion. He drives a Porsche—I think he bought it secondhand from Schwarzenegger—and he's been in Hollywood movies, he's a multimillionaire. He ain't no common man." Humphrey, the advisor says, drives an '89 Oldsmobile station wagon and lives in a modest home. Coleman drives a 1994 Jeep and lives on a regular street in St. Paul. "These guys are more 'common,' " he says, "but because of Jesse's communications skills, he outflanked them."

Coleman agrees, but also says that since he and Skip got tied up in the center of the ring, Jesse was able to shake his head at their scrappy fighting. "I got to engage Humphrey," Coleman says, "and Skip was engaging me, and, in that first debate, people said, 'There go the politicians fighting.' People are tired of the partisan bickering."

The Clinton-Starr brouhaha didn't help matters any, Coleman says. "I don't know if this would have happened at any other time. There was a lot of anger in this country about politics . . . People are mad at Clinton for putting us in this situation where we have to listen to this every day, and at my party for pressing the point. You get someone like Jesse with a message like that and it has some appeal."

"I'm a Skip Humphrey supporter," says former governor Anderson, who watched a few of the gubernatorial debates from beginning to end. "But had I been from another state, and the only thing I had to go on were the debates, I would have voted for Jesse."

"He clearly won the debates running away," the *Strib*'s von Sternberg says. "He gave what people took to be very straight answers."

But von Sternberg, who heard Jesse speak day in and day out, says that Jesse's exemplary debate performances were misleading. "He's got a very limited repertoire, and a very short take on what he can say. After three or four times, it's not so impressive. But most people didn't hear it three or four times, and to them it sounded fresh. And people were just enormously taken with that."

Jesse himself has alluded to his debate romps as coming from somewhere other than a place of intellect. "I'm good in front of the camera," he told MSNBC's John Hockenberry after the election. "My career in wrestling helped tremendously, from being able to do wrestling interviews, making me feel very comfortable in front of a camera. . . . When the red light goes on, I go on."

Sometimes the power of Jesse's charm was literally unbelievable. On October 6, at a debate at Hibbing High School, *Strib* reporter Conrad deFiebre couldn't fathom what he was witnessing.

Hibbing is the hometown of Rudy Perpich, the longest-serving governor in Minnesota history. It is also home to the Iron Range—the region of Minnesota's iron ore mining companies, most of which have been closed down. The area is regarded as mightily strong DFL territory.

Nonetheless, the crowd of 800 Iron Rangers "was just bonkers for Jesse," deFiebre says. "Everything he said, they just went nuts. The response that he got was far and away better than the other two candidates."

Because of the decline of the iron ore industry, the region has been depressed for decades. To counteract the economic sag, the state government established the Iron Range Resources and Rehabilitation Board—the I-triple-B—which sponsors various economic development projects. At one point in the debate, a question was asked about each candidate's support for the I-triple-B.

"The other two said, 'This is something that we support, that we think is very important,'" deFiebre says. But when it came to Jesse's turn, he sang an altogether different tune.

"I don't know anything about it," Jesse said, according to deFiebre, "but it's a government agency, so we oughta look into it, whether or not it should remain. Nowhere in the Constitution does it say government's business is to create jobs. That's the private sector's responsibility.''

The crowd went wild with applause. These were people who had directly, financially benefited—survived, some might say—because of the very institution Jesse was talking about maybe shutting down, though he admitted knowing nothing about it.

''That's absurd, and actually very frightening,'' Coleman replied.

But the crowd wasn't with Coleman. They loved Jesse.

''It was very weird stuff,'' says political scientist Schier. ''There's a lot of thoughtless populism out there, people thinking, 'Ah, if it's government, it can't be any good.' And Jesse taps into that. He spoke for a lot of voters who don't know much about government, but know that they don't like it.''

And they found it refreshing to be told the complete and total truth—regardless of the risk that such blunt honesty would assuredly cost him votes. In St. Cloud over the summer, Jesse had told a room full of transportation officials and highway contractors that he hoped after the Ventura Governorship ended, Minnesotans would say, ''When Jesse Ventura was governor, I don't remember government being around.''[59] It was an extraordinary thing to say to a room full of people who depended on government to live.

It was courage, no doubt. Sure, some said that Jesse could afford to say anything he wanted since he hadn't a ghost of a chance, anyway, but how many politicians stand in front of a group of University of Minnesota students and tell them that if they're smart enough to get into college, they're smart enough to pay for it?

Forget the fact that he was asking for votes, even, how many of us just as people have the confidence to stand at an American Legion post and tell veterans that we oppose a flag-burning amendment, which Jesse did?

"You're not going to necessarily like my answer," he told the vet who asked him the question that day. "The point is we have the freedom to do something like that, people—the flag's only the symbol." Besides, Jesse noted, flag burners usually get the shit kicked out of them by construction workers, anyway.

It wasn't so surprising—especially in the year of the Clinton-Starr spin wars—that people were connecting to him.

The pattern continued, debate after debate. At October 16 in Duluth, Jesse reminded voters that he was the only candidate who refused PAC money. "Jesse Ventura is not owned by special interest groups," he said. "My two opponents can't say that. They're not leading by example . . . For what it is, November third is no longer an election, it's an auction."

Behind the appealing populism, Jesse's platform and pronouncements were erratic and short on specifics. "I have never advocated a tax cut," he insisted at one press conference while his Website said, simultaneously, "I support lowering residential property taxes and the state income tax."

He was short on specifics, big on sports metaphors. "I want to go back after government," he said in response to a question about the budget. "I want to get in there and get my hands in there and find out where the pork is," he said, lifting his hands as if holding the entire bureaucracy in a choke hold. Sometimes he seemed to think that the rules didn't apply to him, that there was no reason that he should, say, offer a budget plan—even while he was criticizing his opponents' plans.

Are you ever going to offer a budget plan? he was asked.

"Oh, it could happen," he said.

When?

"I dunno—I'm busy running," he said.

Wasn't it patently unfair to bash his rival's plans when he hadn't come up with one himself?

"Is there anything fair in politics?" he'd ask. "Hey, I have every right to run for governor—I'm qualified."[60]

For their parts, Humphrey and Coleman pretty much ignored Jesse. I'm the only candidate out here who has cut taxes, Coleman would say, and Humphrey's going to tax you into oblivion. Humphrey would counterpunch: I'm the only candidate up here who's offered a budget plan, he would say, following that up with various slams against his Republican opponent. They'd tear at each other, punching each other's buttons, getting under one another's skins with shrillness and whining and negativity.

Jesse, on the other hand, said whatever came to mind. "Jesse had the freedom that comes from no financial support from anybody," former Governor Anderson says. "Because clearly no special interests were supporting him. He didn't have to worry about focus groups, commercials—his mind wasn't cluttered by advice from experts and consultants. . . . And nobody took Jesse on, including the press."

That wasn't how Jesse saw it, though. Especially not after October 21, when the biggest controversy of his political career erupted.

SEVENTEEN

"ABSOLUTELY NOT."

Some libertarian beliefs—less government, lower taxes, more personal freedoms—are popular across the political spectrum.

Some are more controversial, like the argument that the government has no right to restrict who can purchase a firearm. Or even who has the legal right to carry around a loaded firearm on their person at all times.

(During his campaign, Jesse would argue against gun control and complain that even he, as mayor, had been denied a permit to carry a concealed weapon by his police chief. Former chief Davis, however, says that this bit of Jesse lore stretches the truth. First, Jesse had applied for the permit to carry a concealed weapon before he was mayor. Second, Davis hadn't denied him the permit—the law had. Minnesota's concealed-weapon law only allows common citizens to walk around with loaded handguns at the quick if they need one for their job or if there is a compelling personal safety issue—and Jesse didn't fit the requirements.)

Still other libertarian arguments—the legalization of drugs and prostitution foremost among them—are the political equivalent of a request for a house call from Dr. Kevorkian.

On Wednesday, October 21, Jesse appeared before

a Forest Lake business association when he was asked if he favored legalizing drugs or prostitution. Rather politically, Jesse said that he had "never once stated that I wanted to legalize" either one.

But then he went on.

"I'm not for legalizing prostitution," he said, "but it's legal in Nevada. And they don't seem to have any major problems going on there with it. My point is, I don't want to imprison these people. . . . I would rather imprison people that are going to harm you and me, not someone who harms themself. Ladies and gentleman, you cannot legislate stupidity. People are going to do stupid things. We cannot sit and every time someone does something stupid, make it a law and have the government come in, because if you do that, you're going to lose your freedom. . . . Freedom is what's important."

Reporters at the edge of the room immediately smelled something . . . What was it? (sniff, sniff) . . . Was it a story? Was it blood?

"My ears perked up," says WCCO-TV's Pat Kessler. Jesse had advocated legalizing prostitution "only about 800 times on his radio talk show, so this was not new to me, but it was new to me his being this candid during the campaign."

As Jesse walked out of the forum, Kessler stuck a mike in his face.

"Are you talking about legalizing prostitution?" Kessler asked

"Well, it might be something to look at," Jesse replied. "I don't know necessarily if I'd like it. But I think I'm the type of person that I'm open-minded enough, to where I think I'd like to look at different situations like that. I'll put it to you this way: It's a lot easier to control something when it's legal than when it's illegal. . . . And you know, maybe (if) I also took a trip to Amsterdam and saw how they deal with it. And they keep it in one part of the city and if you don't desire to see it or participate, you don't go there.''

''So is that something you'd support?'' Kessler pressed.

''I don't know that I'd support it, Pat, but it's something certainly we should look at. You know, in the aspect of getting it out of the neighborhoods. I mean, one of the biggest concerns right now are porno shops in the neighborhoods. Well, we have, you know, the First Amendment. We have freedom. Why not find a place to put 'em all? You know, and that way you keep them out of the neighborhood. You know, find a spot where they can locate this kind of thing. Let's talk about it. The porno industry is a multi-billion-dollar industry. So it's not something only a few people are taking part in.''

''So, in this area prostitutes would not be arrested?'' Kessler asked, trying to understand just what exactly Jesse was proposing.

''Uh, I don't know,'' Jesse said, backing off. ''You know, I'm not going to go on the record right now, but I'm just going to—''

''You are on the record,'' Kessler reminded him.

''Yeah, I'm on the record,'' he said. ''But I just don't want to get people all panicked, because I know how they take things out of context. But I think we need to look at solving these social problems in a different manner than what we have now. Because what we're doing now is not progressive. It's not working.''

As soon as his opponents heard what Jesse had said, they opened fire.

''That is one of the most absurd and outrageous propositions I have heard in the entire course of this campaign," Coleman said when told of Jesse's comments. "The people of Minnesota should be outraged; they should be frightened."

It's "a terrible message to women, young and old, and to children," Humphrey said.

But reporters seemed more upset than voters. "That thud you just heard was Jesse Ventura plunging in the polls," the *Brainerd Dispatch* opined in an editorial, incorrectly and prematurely. Jesse "has won favor with voters who clearly are turned off by government as usual," the newspaper continued. "But even though these people say they favor Ventura now, there is a strong suspicions that once they are in the voting booth they will mark their preference for either the Democrat of Republican. They are apt to remember what he said or didn't say about prostitution and whatever other controversy arises between now and election day."

To Jesse, the *Brainerd Dispatch*'s overblown—and, of course, embarrassingly wrong—pronouncement was typical. Reporters were no better than the career politicians—out-of-touch, elitist, frequently at odds with the common joe.

Still Jesse backed off from what he had said. "I was misquoted Wednesday," he insisted. "When asked if I supported legalized prostitution and drugs, the first two words I said were, 'Absolutely not.' "

Not so, says KSTP's Jason Lewis. "Jesse said, 'That's not what I said.' But that *is* what he said."

Perhaps to Jesse's credit, he'd given a much more thoughtful response than just "Absolutely not." And a more honest one. After all, how many politicians—Bill Clinton, Al Gore, Newt Gingrich—had smoked pot as young adults yet later, as politicians, publicly opposed drug legalization?

But the press kept making a big deal out of his comments on prostitution. TV, radio, newspapers . . . The next day he came out and announced that he had been misquoted, and reiterated that he would "absolutely not" support legalization of the world's oldest profession—though he also restated that Minnesota needed to start considering new solutions. Again, he delivered a confusing attempt to have it both ways.

"He was never misquoted," says Kessler, who has the entire exchange on videotape. "It became clear that if [Jesse and his campaign] attacked the media, they would generally gain some ground if they made mistakes."

Deciphering the following statement, for instance, which he made in a radio interview, is near impossible—as the two sentences are in complete contradiction.

"Jesse Ventura is not going to legalize prostitution in any way, shape, or form," he said. "I'm open-minded to look at other alternative methods of dealing with it, like the state of Nevada."

"He's hanging his hat on a technicality," Kessler says. "While he many times in many ways advocated the legalization of prostitution [on his radio show] while he was a candidate he'd always hang on a qualifier, saying that 'Minnesota ought to consider it.' "

Jesse had made a similarly confusing policy statement on marijuana legalization to the pro-pot *High Times* in an interview published right before the election. "Let's not talk about whether to make it legal or illegal," he said. "Let's talk about the monetary potential. Why aren't we taxing it? I say tax the hell out of it. Then lower my taxes." While candid and honest, the fact is that the government can't tax marijuana as long as it's illegal. Such a statement makes no sense.

Kessler says that the hair-splitting on pot or hookers or "No New Taxes" or whatever are the smaller issues. "He's no different from other politicians in this regard," Kessler says. "The inconsistency is that he says he's not."

It didn't seem to matter, though. Minnesotans knew that no governor would ever be able to legalize prostitution, even if he wanted to. It was just Jesse being Jesse, many of them thought. Shortly after the prostitution brouhaha, a poll revealed that Jesse was still only gaining popularity.

But Jesse didn't let it go so simply. It infuriated him that the media could attack him, go after him, so tenaciously, so mercilessly. So eagerly. Why didn't they like him? he wondered.

His opponents, on the other hand, saw Jesse and the media as hand-in-hand. Jesse was a media creation, they thought, and reporters let him get away with murder.

"We put together a budget plan that we worked on for a long time," says Coleman. "It was very sustainable, calculating potential drops in the economy, dealing with different rates in inflation. And even that got taken apart. . . . Jesse didn't have a tax plan, but it didn't matter. In that sense, was there a different standard? Yeah, but talk to the media about that."

"He wasn't really scrutinized or even given a look by the media," says a source in the Humphrey campaign. "For sure, Jesse was given a free ride by the media."

Jesse didn't think so. He was pissed off when it came down to endorsement time. The *Strib* and the St. Paul *Pioneer Press* didn't even give him a chance, he thought. He saw the same arrogance in the editorial boards that he saw in the state legislatures. They were unaccountable, they didn't think like real people.

"I get better treatment nationally than I do from the local press, I don't know why," he told MSNBC's Hockenberry.

At the end of October, that statement seemed true on its face. The national press swept in for glowing stories that could have been written and produced by Friedline and Barkley. On October 25, *ABC World News Tonight* ran a segment on Jesse; on October 26, CNN's *Inside Politics* followed suit; on October 27, NBC's *Today Show* did so, as did NPR'S *Morning Edition* on October 28.

Media-folk in Minnesota weren't on the bandwagon. Endorsements started trickling in. Humphrey secured the support of the editorial boards of the *Star Tribune*, Mankato's *Free Press*, and the *St. Cloud Times*. Coleman received the backing of the St. Paul *Pioneer Press*, the Mesabi *Daily News*, Austin *Daily Herald*, and *The Journal of New Ulm*.

Not one newspaper endorsed Jesse. It bothered him. Politicians work best once they develop thick skins to withstand criticism and attacks. Jesse wasn't like that. He was almost childishly sensitive sometimes.

"He's thin-skinned," says the *Strib*'s von Sternberg. "He does not have a good sense of humor about himself and he's real quick to take offense. . . . When something pisses him off, he lets you know it under no uncertain terms. A couple times I was interviewing him one-on-one and *BAM* he was in my face. And you don't get that [often from politicians], somebody teeing off in your face."

Specifically, one of Jesse's rants against von Sternberg concerned the *Strib*'s attempts to learn more about the gubernatorial candidate's activities during the Vietnam War. "He was furious by the fact that somebody was able to get his records, and he just lit in,'' von Sternberg says.

Jesse's former KSTP colleague, Jason Lewis, was probably Jesse's harshest critic. "I was pretty tough on him," Lewis says. But, he points out, "a lot of people treated him unfairly by going after his professional background, going after his intellect. I never did that—I treated him like a candidate, going after him on the issues."

Jesse's statements were actually a different style of "the classic political machinations," according to Lewis, "the ultimate in career politics." He was on all sides of many issues. A state bonding bill, for instance, included government funding for construction of a hockey stadium in St. Paul—the Minnesota Wild were slated to come in 2001. Lewis opposed government help for the hockey arena, as did Jesse. "But Jesse when he was on KFAN was a big supporter of bailing out the Target Center . . ." The difference? Jesse's an NBA Timberwolves fan—and that's the team that plays at the Target Center.

"He would take these contradictory positions all the time and I would merely point them out and Jesse didn't like that," Lewis says. "This civil libertarian thought that the FDA should regulate tobacco." The inconsistency "comes from a place of arrogance," says Lewis. When Lewis and Jesse would debate these issues when they were both at KSTP, Jesse's response was, according to his former rival, '' 'sure I'm inconsistent but it's how I feel, and it's how I feel so it's right.' ''

EIGHTEEN

THE AIR WAR

Out in Pillager, Minnesota, Buford Johnson—vice chair of Minnesota's Reform Party—was one of the few people in the state confident that Jesse would win. He even bet a friend not only that the former pro-wrestler would win, but would do so by more than five percentage points.

Johnson was so sure because of what was happening with his supply of *Ventura for Governor* signs. Volunteers kept coming up to him for more and more, and he kept running out, so he soon started telling them to make their own. They did. Soon you couldn't drive anywhere without seeing dozens of these hand-made signs scattered on lawns throughout the area.

But even though the momentum was with Jesse, back at the Ventura/Schunk campaign, the staff was worried that no matter how well Jesse was doing, in the end it wouldn't be enough. Garnering the next ten to twenty percentage points necessary to snag the plu-rality victory, that was going to be tough, if not im-possible, they thought. Humphrey had wised up and had started backing out of debates. Jesse knew that in order to get the attention and popularity his campaign needed, he would need cash to run TV ads.

But the campaign was broke. And neither the na-tional Reform Party or its megalomaniacal founder, billionaire Ross Perot, were coughing up a dime. There was a subtext to Perot's indifference. Many Reform Party activists from Minnesota had backed Perot's opponent for the '96 nomination, former Colorado Governor Dick Lamm. Plus, many Reform Party activists whispered, there was no way Perot would ever support the rise of a candidate other than himself.

And while Perot twiddled his thumbs and counted his coin out in Texas, the Democratic and Republican parties shuttled in their big guns to raise funds for their men in Minnesota. On October 12, Vice President Al Gore came to Minneapolis to stump and raise money at campaign events for Skip. "I'm really glad to be here to brag on Skip Humphrey," Gore said. "This is really an exciting ticket." U.S. Secretary of Agriculture Dan Glickman came to help Skip on October 22.

A commensurate effort was made for Coleman by the Republican Party. The GOP's '96 Vice Presidential candidate, Jack Kemp, appeared at a St. Paul charter school with Coleman on October 21, and the other man on 1996's losing ticket, Presidential nominee Bob Dole, stumped for the St. Paul mayor the next day.

Compared to Coleman and Humphrey, Jesse's campaign was downright broke. Even when it came to the public money they were all due because of the state's public financing laws. The state's public financing laws would distribute $2.4 million from the state's general fund to 259 candidates that year, Coleman and Skip included—but not until the election was over. Typically, campaigns would secure loans from banks for the amount they would get after the election—Coleman's campaign, for instance, had no problem getting a loan for the $559,639 public subsidy it had coming, nor did Humphrey have much trouble getting someone to spot his campaign $603,544. Jesse was due $326,821 of that sum, but as of early October, his campaign's loan applications for that amount had already been turned down by a half-dozen banks.

Bob Maline, Jesse's campaign's treasurer, was frustrated. Maline, a thirty-six-year-old former DFL delegate and production supervisor for the 3M Corporation, had been turned down by twenty-five banks and mortgage companies. He'd even gone to Lloyd's of London, which had rejected Maline's proposal that Lloyd's insure against Jesse's getting 5% of vote.

Finally, Maline found an Illinois company willing to give the insurance policy idea a shot. Before that went through, however, a member of the Minneapolis city council suggested that Maline try Franklin National Bank, a small institution with only eighteen employees. Franklin National approved. Loan officer Jim Shadko was amazed to learn that Jesse's campaign only spent money it actually had, money it had raised that week—budgeting as taught by Bernice Janos.

(After the election, Shadko was also stunned when the loan was repaid the very day it was due. Such promptness was not strictly necessary, but Jesse's campaign took pride in fiscal responsibility.)

While Maline had been busying himself with the money hunt, Barkley focused on what the cash would ultimately be spent on—the TV and radio ads. It was only natural that he would decide to hire and leave the creative decisions to Bill Hillsman.

Hillsman, forty-five, was a fixture in Minneapolis' small but nationally acclaimed world of advertising, having owned a local commercial ad agency. Hillsman had made his bones, however, in political advertising, coming up with the groundbreaking 1990 ads for Paul Wellstone's first senate race.

The Wellstone ads were funny and memorable. One was called "Fast-Paced Paul." The conceit behind it was that underdog Wellstone was underfunded and had to speed-talk in order to fit everything he wanted to say into a thirty-second spot. Another ad, "Looking for Rudy," was longer, a two-minute ad based on Michael Moore's populist documentary *Roger and Me*. In the ad, Wellstone traveled throughout the state looking for his opponent, incumbent GOP Senator Rudy Boschwitz, who had initially refused to debate his scrappy challenger.

The ads got a lot of notice—some said they revolutionized political advertising. Hillsman received a lot of the credit for Wellstone's surprising upset victory. The ads garnered major awards from the advertising, political consulting, and marketing industries.

Since then, Hillsman had scored a few victories—most notably with Sharon Sayles-Belton, the first African-American and the first woman to be elected Mayor of Minneapolis, in 1992. But, with a number of commercials for some high-profile duds, it had been awhile since he scored a big victory in state. (Ads he did for Perot in '92 were never used.)

At the beginning of 1998, Hillsman had bet on another losing horse, signing up with DFL gubernatorial candidate Doug Johnson, a moderate state senator who may have been the only non-famous name in that race. Two reporters Hillsman knew suggested that, if Johnson didn't win, the ad man should sign up with Jesse's campaign. "I don't know if they wanted to make the race more interesting, or what," Hillsman says.

Johnson did, of course, lose—though he exceeded all expectations, tying for second place though he'd trailed in the polls. Barkley and Friedline liked the parallels. In early October, Hillsman got together with them. He knew Barkley from his other races and liked him a lot—"Dean's a credit to politicians, he's a stand-up guy," Hillsman says.

Hillsman also had a favorable impression of Jesse, having run into him in January, 1991, on the tarmac bidding farewell to Minnesota National Guardsmen heading off to fight Operation Desert Storm. "Paul [Wellstone] did it, certainly, because it was the right thing to do, but also because it was a photo opportunity," Hillsman says.

"Jesse was there . . . because it was the right thing to do. I remember thinking, 'This guy is not the kind of one-dimensional character people make him out to be.' It was one of those impressions you get and then think, 'Hmm,' and file it away and think nothing of it for years and years." Then in '98, he'd seen Jesse perform in the DFL debates and was impressed.

On Sunday, October 4, Hillsman met Jesse's chief advisors at Barkley's house to talk about what he had learned working for Johnson and how he could use that knowledge on his new job working for Jesse. They looked at the counties where Doug Johnson had done well, thinking they would be where Jesse's DFL votes would come from.

But though they were all discussing Johnson's campaign, it was another candidate whom Hillsman was thinking about. "You could see a groundswell of support for Jesse," he says, "I got the same feeling that I got with Wellstone in '90." On October 9, the Ventura/Schunk campaign announced that Hillsman—and his marketing, communications, and political consulting firm, North Woods Advertising—had come on board.

Occasionally Hillsman would use employees at the consumer ad agency where he was a partner—Krus-

kopf Olson Advertising, or KO—on a freelance basis.
With only fourteen employees, KO had built a name
for itself by making daring ads for smaller clients, providing a big bang of innovation for not many bucks.
A typical piece, for a pet food store, showed a cat
having a psychedelic episode. "Catnip is still legal in
all fifty states . . . and it's one of the many products
available at Pet Food Warehouse," the ad went.

KO's emphasis on creativity "really separates our
work from the average, annoying commercials you see
every day," says Bill Whitney, the firm's thirty-year-
old artistic director. KO makes a point, he says, of
"hooking up with clients who are willing to take
chances, and not take the familiar routes and do the
safe and conservative advertising. . . . With a small
budget, you can make a huge splash—if you are willing to open yourself up to some unusual ideas."

At 5:30 PM, on Friday, October 9, Hillsman sat and
met with Whitney, forty-one-year-old president and
creative director Susan Kruskopf, management supervisor Jean Koelz, and copywriters Dan Mackaman and
Beth Kinney. The six-person team piled into KO's one
conference room to talk about Jesse's commercials—
ideas which Hillsman needed to present to the campaign after the weekend.

"The good thing was that the agency was really
into it because Jesse was the kind of candidate we
were really into, and the kind of guy who would understand the kind of advertising we wanted to try,"
Kruskopf says. Which helped, considering the fact that
when they sat down that Friday evening, it was still
unclear that Ventura/Schunk was going to receive its
$330,000 public financing. "It takes time to develop
good ideas," Kruskopf says. "We were really concerned that we weren't going to have enough time, so

we started before we knew for sure that the money was going to come in.''

Hillsman "gave us the background on where Jesse was, and copies of articles about Jesse," Kinney recalls. Hillsman told them that the campaign "had to target young males at that point—what we considered Jesse's biggest audience—and he briefed us on Jesse's platform.'' The meeting broke up and the team got to work.

Friday and Saturday, Whitney and Kinney, twenty-seven, "read tons of articles and took tons of notes," she says. We "got together over the weekend and just jammed on this thing totally,'' says Whitney. Neither one of them had ever worked on any political advertising before. Mackaman, thirty-four, worked on the radio scripts, as he had for Johnson's campaign during the DFL primary. All three of them were nervous but excited.

The six-person team went into the office on Sunday at noon and sat around the room brainstorming. Their candidate—the product—was more unique and unusual than any other product they'd ever tried to sell before. They needed to come up with ads that captured just exactly how fresh Jesse was. Something really wild.

They sat down. Between them, they had about twenty ideas: eight for radio, ten for TV, and a couple for newspaper ads.

They were out there, for sure. "The same ads for Skip Humphrey wouldn't have worked," says Kinney. "But if you had done mundane ads for Jesse, it would have seemed like the wrong tone. . . . You couldn't build him into something that he wasn't. The ads were almost metaphorical of who he was.''

The TV ideas were the most important, of course.

One of the team's ideas was a reverse on Superman—
Jesse, in his Champlin Park High School coaching
duds, would run into a phone booth and come out in
a three-piece suit. But filming such an ad would have
taken an entire day of Jesse's time, time he didn't have
to spare from the campaign trail. That one was nixed.

Another idea involved the idea of a Jesse Ventura
action figure. There were a few permutations of that
brainstorm—one had a Navy SEAL frogman suit you
could put on the doll to reenact Jesse's adventures in
'Nam—and, sold separately, you could buy the Norm
and Skip tea-party set. Hillsman liked the idea of the
action figure, though he wasn't sure about going negative on Norm and Skip.

One print ad possibility from the first round de-
picted Jesse as Rodin's "The Thinker," contrasting
Jesse "The Body" with his new incarnation, Jesse
"The Mind." Hillsman looked at it. He liked it.
"Let's make this a TV spot," he said.

Hillsman took the ideas, finessed them, and presented them to Friedline, and Barkley. Hillsman had
also come up with an idea for the last weekend of the
campaign—Jesse's Seventy-two Hour Drive to Victory. "I'd actually stolen the idea from Bob Dole,"
Hillsman admits. "But that idea didn't make much
sense for a seventy-two-year-old guy, it always struck
me as stupid for Dole" since it only emphasized his
lack of vigor. "But for a guy like Jesse—a macho guy,
with a lot of feeling, and a lot of momentum" it made
sense.

The radio ads were taped and hit the airwaves. The
TV ads were filmed a few days later and were up and
running by the next week. They were a huge hit.

The radio ads were cute and funny. One had Jesse
talking about the issues he believed in, concluding

with his observation that "I believe that Led Zeppelin and the Rolling Stones are two of the best rock bands of all time." Another one, which hit the airwaves on October 20, had a campaign theme song which sounded more than a little like Isaac Hayes's "Theme from *Shaft*," complete with cooing backup singers ("Ooooh, Jesse!") complementing Jesse's machismo: "When the other guys were cashing government checks, he was in the Navy getting dirty and wet," a singer grooved; "You're making me blush," said Jesse.

But the TV ads were the big hit. Ventura/Schunk didn't have the budget—and couldn't afford the delay—to order an actual "Jesse Ventura action figure," so Whitney, account person Koelz, and commercial director Mark Carter scampered throughout the city cruising toy stores, grocery stores, K-Marts, and Walgreens looking for any dolls even remotely Jesse-like. They ended up using the tinkered-with head of an Omar Bradley GI Joe Special Issue doll that Whitney had found, the body of DC comics' *Nightwing* which Carter had scored, and the suit of a Ken Doll, snagged by Koelz.

(Carter had also brought back a WWF "Stone Cold" Steve Austin action figure, but " 'Stone Cold' looked kind of crazy," Whitney says, while "Omar Bradley had a much more statesman-like quality." Whitney also bought a James Dean doll that was going to double as Norm Coleman, and a James Bond villain doll to be Skip. But Jesse's campaign decided not to go directly negative against his opponents.)

Soon the ad was up and on the air, just in time for the last two weeks of the campaign.

"New! From the Reform Party! It's the new Jesse Ventura action figure!" the narrator gushed as two kids played with the action figure. "You can make Jesse battle special interest groups . . ."

"I don't want your stupid money!" said the kid with the Jesse doll, to the kid with the Evil Special Interest Man doll (a converted Ken doll.)

". . . and party politics!" said the narrator.

"We politicians have powers the average man can't comprehend!" said the kid with the Evil Special Interest Man doll.

"You can also make Jesse lower taxes, improve public education, and fight for the things Minnesotans really care about!"

"This bill wastes taxpayer money! Re-draft it!" yelled the kid with the Jesse doll, making "Jesse" pound a desk angrily.

"Don't waste your vote on politics as usual!" the ad concluded. "Vote Reform Party candidate Jesse Ventura for governor!"

The "Thinker" ad—called "Jesse The Mind"— had also been chosen—which made everyone a little nervous. "It was a really unusual type of thing," Whitney says. Jesse was to be sitting there in Rodin's famous sculptural pose, in his shorts, almost naked. They wondered if it was too provocative in the Clinton-Lewinsky era.

A body double was dispatched to the scene for most of the filming—Jesse didn't have a day to give up, and the double—Raymond "JR" Bonus, a gym owner from Roseville—was in better shape. A year before at KFAN, the forty-seven-year-old Jesse had been taking a ribbing from a colleague who'd dubbed him Jesse "The Belly" Ventura. Jesse "said he's 250" pounds, said Bonus, "but I'm 260 and that thing they had me sitting on turning—it was dragging with him on it" when Jesse came in for close-ups. "The motor didn't want to run."[61]

The "Jesse The Mind" ad hit the airwaves in the last week of the campaign.

"THE BODY," read the screen as a voice-over read a list of Jesse's accomplishments. The screen showed a stark brown-and-white image of Jesse (or Bonus) in the "Thinker" pose, with quick MTV cuts of his (or Bonus's) knees, arms, pectorals, and shaved head.

"Navy SEAL. Union member. Volunteer high school football coach. Outdoorsman. Husband of twenty-three years. Father of two."

Then the screen read: "THE MIND".

"A man who will fight to return Minnesota's budget surplus to the taxpayers," said the narrator. "Who will fight to lower property and income taxes. Who does not accept money from special interest groups. And who will work to improve public schools by reducing class sizes."

"JESSE VENTURA OUR NEXT GOVERNOR," read the screen, opera music in the background. Then the camera closed in on the candidate. He smiled softly and winked.

"We shot a bunch of different endings," Whitney says. "One where he kept a stoic face, another when he cracked a smile, another when he broke the pose, taking his arm down. But the wink was a charming thing, and really just broke the seriousness of the spot. It showed he could joke with himself, 'Hey, I'm not so serious.' A lot of women liked it, we had a lot of positive messages on the message board on the Website."

"The Hillsman ads put an exclamation point on the whole thing," says Buck Humphrey.

But would it be enough?

"Two weeks before the election, one of the most respected political reporters in the state told me, 'This is not a serious campaign. This guy doesn't know what he's talking about,' " reports political scientist Schier.

The public was coming to the exact opposite conclusion. According to one poll—sponsored by Minnesota Public Radio, KARE 11 and the *Pioneer Press*—Jesse was winning converts amazingly quickly. On October 14, Humphrey had 44%, Coleman 31, and Jesse 15. Two weeks later, on October 29, Humphrey's numbers had sunk to 34%, Coleman had increased a little bit, to 34% and Jesse had shot up to 23.

"As it began to get crazier," says the *Strib*'s von Sternberg, "we decided we gotta stick to this guy like glue."

"Well, Coach. I'm doing what you said," Jesse told his old high school teacher and football coach "Mac" McInroy at a Roosevelt High School football game toward the end of October. "I didn't like how things were being run, so now I got my hat in the ring. And when the odds are against you, you got to find a way to win."

"Yeah, just like football game," Mac said, "If you can't go down the middle, go around the side."

"We're going right down through the middle, Coach," Jesse said.

The last gubernatorial debate was held on Friday, October 30, and Jesse was outspoken and brash. When asked about government involvement in preschool preparation, Jesse chastised anyone who expected schools to raise kids. "That's called parenting," he said. When asked about using taxpayer dollars for funding a new stadium for the Twins, Jesse said that "When Mike Plazza"—the catcher for the New York Mets—"signs for $91 million for seven years, they can build their own damn stadium."

EIGHTEEN

THE GROUND WAR

On the "Thursday before election day, the election depends less on the media and more on literature drops and work in the field," says Hillsman. "It's not an air war anymore—it becomes a ground war." Jesse and his team took the ground.

Jesse, media man, kicked off his seventy-two-hour Drive To Victory Tour at KTCA-TV, Channel 2 in St. Paul, and then headed to a bunch of sports bars in the northern suburbs of the Twin Cities—Champps, New Brighton Eagles Club, Mermaid Bar, and the BeBop Bar—for twenty-minute walk-throughs. "We spent that last weekend chasing him all over the state," says von Sternberg. "The first thing he did was hit a bunch of bars where he got a tremendous response. Thousands of people jammed the bars. Friedline was just flabbergasted."

All weekend, Jesse and Dean and Doug were amazed at the positive response out there. It hadn't all been for naught, they realized. They were reaching people. The debates, the ads, the hours of strategizing—they hadn't been just screaming in the woods.

Jesse paraded around in casual clothes—a SEALs T-shirt, a Timberwolves jacket, an unlit cigar in his hand—and Minnesotans loved him. They surrounded him, shaking his hand and pledging their votes and their family's votes and their friends' votes. Jesse was no stranger to celebrity, but this was something else entirely—people acted like they had confidence in him, as if they knew Jesse would be their salvation. No one was more stunned than the candidate himself.

For any campaign, the added burden of the last few days of an election is not only to continue to generate interest in its candidate, but to motivate its voters to get their asses to the polls to vote. The Democratic and Republican parties had the organization of men and women out in the real world who would make sure that the party faithful would get motivated to pull the levers.

The Reform Party didn't have field organizers. Instead they had the Internet.

"After every election cycle, you hear some buzz about the hot new thing, and I'd been hearing about the Internet for years," says Hillsman. In the past, though, Web-heads proved themselves to be "computer geeky white males who tend not to show up at polls," Hillsman says. But those were Jesse voters, and www.jesseventura.org proved a huge success, raising more campaign contributions and volunteers than any other campaign Website nationwide.

"This was the first time it worked," Hillsman says. "It basically substituted for any sort of field organization." The site, launched in February, "was filled with information," Hillsman says, particularly during Jesse's seventy-two-hour Drive to Victory Tour. "Jesse's Geek Squad" provided the site with up-to-the-minute information of where the caravan was. They produced video clips and digital photos of the caravan and rallies and immediately transmitted them to the Website as soon as they got to a phone line.

"Without the Internet we would have lost the election," Jesse's webmaster, Phil Madsen, would later say. The President of *PoliticsOnline* called Jesse the "JFK of the Net," comparing his successful use of the Web with Senator John F. Kennedy's effective use of television during his 1960 run for the Presidency.

On Saturday, October 31, the caravan was scheduled to hit a truck stop in downtown Anoka, and St. Cloud State University. Jesse took a time out to run into a supermarket to check on the prices of milk and frozen turkey—in a recent debate, he and his opponents had been asked how much those items cost and not one of them had any idea.

That day the *Strib* released the last poll of the campaign season. The race was a statistical dead heat: Humphrey was at 35%, Coleman at 30, and Jesse at 27—well within striking distance. Von Sternberg showed the poll results to Jesse and Friedline. "They were just stunned," he says. "A couple times in the previous weeks he'd let his guard drop, and said, 'Oh, I'm not gonna win this, though it's been fun.' The poll just shocked him."

Most significantly, the poll indicated that Jesse was the favorite of younger voters, ages eighteen to twenty-four, who favored Jesse overwhelmingly, by 45% as opposed to Coleman's 27% and Humphrey's 16. While the numbers were not as staggeringly high, Jesse held a plurality over Skip and Norm among *all* voters under the age of forty-five.

"However," the *Strib* concluded, "the youngest voters are often the least likely to make it to the polls." That day Secretary of State Joan Growe—the first candidate whom Jesse had ever really supported for office, back in the seventies, announced her estimation that 53% of the state's 3,483,000 voters would turn out to vote. If she was right, it probably wouldn't be enough for Jesse to win.

"The election Tuesday is not about empty promises or entertaining sideshows," First Lady Hillary Rodham Clinton said that day—in a clear swipe at Jesse—as she stumped for Skip.

"Sideshow, eh?" Jesse mumbled to friends. *Maybe the First Lady should spend a little more time in Washington and a little less in Minnesota,* Jesse said. *It's when she goes out of town that her husband seemed to get into trouble.*

That night, the Champlin Park High school football team faced off against Anoka High in its run for the state championship. Jesse was there, assistant-coaching, cheering, lending his support. Champlin High won. The caravan spent Sunday in southern Minnesota and Monday in the Iron Range.

"The night before the election," Wendell Anderson recounts, "I went to a grocery store and the young man working there"—a faithful DFLer—"said, 'Governor Anderson, give me some good news! I talked to ten people today and nine of them are voting for Jesse.'"

The next day, Anderson would run into a Republican ward leader and he would say the same thing. "Everybody's voting for Jesse!" he exclaimed, befuddled.

"We were getting the vote out," Buck Humphrey says, "and we were driving people to the polls to get the vote out for dad." One Humphrey van was packed with Carleton College students—all of whom were voting for Jesse.

People were flocking—stampeding—to vote. Out in Todd County, voter turnout was so high the precincts ran out of their supply of printed ballots—even though they'd prepared for an 80% voter turnout. First-time and previously disillusioned voters were coming out of the woodwork. Minnesota voters can register to vote on election day itself, and an election judge would later tell Buck that there were five times the number of people in the registration lines than in voting lines.

By the time the polls closed that night, Minnesota had secured the national first place slot for voter turnout. The national average for that day was 37%.

In Minnesota, it was 61%.

And for every point that voter turnout exceeded 53%—those voters whom the Secretary of State anticipated would come out—the odds that Jesse might actually pull this off increased exponentially. They were the young, the disenfranchised, the men and women usually either too pissed-off or too indifferent to vote. A lot of them turned out that day. And they were voting for Jesse.

That night, Jesse, his campaign staff and friends and family all traveled southwest of the Twin Cities to watch the returns come in at Canterbury Park racetrack—a place where longshots occasionally come in.

Jesse, Terry, and others were drinking and laughing in a back room at Canterbury Park. The reception area was packed with so many young men it looked almost like fraternity rush. Or a pro wrestling meet.

Jesse and his crew didn't think that he was going to win, so they were more interested in partying than in watching the returns come in. Hillsman—annoyed by their noise—went upstairs to the media room to get the numbers. Doug and Dean shuttled back and forth between the back room and the floor of the reception area.

At five PM, exit polls came in, and they looked exactly like the polls taken before election day. Humphrey led with 37%. Norm Coleman was right behind him, at 34, and Jesse brought up the rear with a respectable 29. Another exit poll followed, and that showed the same result. But then a third exit poll came out—one that factored in all those late voters lined up to register—and Jesse was actually in the lead.

Soon after the polls closed at eight, 9% of the vote—the *actual* vote, not polls—came in, and Jesse was in first place, having amassed 37%.

The crowd was going wild. They formed a mosh pit and started body-surfing

"He can't stay there," Hillsman said to himself. "It's going to slide back down."

Over at Coleman's victory party, at the Radison in downtown St. Paul, mouths were agape. In the last week of the campaign, Coleman's pollsters had taken the temperature of 200 voters every night. There were a couple nights that Jesse had beaten Skip, but he never passed Norm. They all had figured that "in the end, he was a third-party candidate, and their voters either don't show up, or they vote for someone else," according to Coleman. The last poll the Coleman campaign had taken, the day before the election, Coleman beat Humphrey by five or so points.

The Humphrey folks were similarly stunned. "Our very last poll in that last week had us ahead of Norm by one point," says the Humphrey advisor. "Jesse had not broken twenty."

"None of that reflected Jesse's ability to win new voters and to bring people to the polls," Coleman says. Pollsters regularly screen out voters who haven't voted in the last few elections, since they usually continue their habit of apathy. So the polls didn't reflect the men and women Jesse was energizing.

At Skip Humphrey's victory ball, at the Hilton Hotel in downtown Minneapolis, the mood was downright funereal. "Everybody was in disbelief," says Buck. "We all had this numb feeling, like 'What the *hell* just happened?' For upwards of two years, we'd been working for one goal, to make my father the governor. We did everything we possibly could."

They remained optimistic. "That probably doesn't include the Iron Range and some rural areas where we'll come in stronger," the Humphrey advisor recalls saying. "Let's wait for more numbers."

With 30% of the vote in, Jesse was still holding steady at 37. Jesse entered the room. His supporters went nuts. Complete pandemonium. He got up behind the podium. He was afraid that his lead wouldn't hold and that the crowd would be disappointed.

"It's all yours!" a man yelled.

"We're a third of the way around the track," said Jesse.

"Bring it home, Jesse!" shouted another.

Jesse went back to the private room.

With 58% of the vote in, Jesse was holding strong with 37 and the local CBS affiliate put a checkmark next to Jesse's name.

Jesse couldn't believe it.

"There's still 40% of the vote not counted!" he said. "How can they call me the winner when they still haven't counted 40% of the vote?!"

He thought of "Dewey defeats Truman." He didn't want to go out there and declare victory when there was, in his mind, still a good chance that he was going to lose. He didn't want to look like an idiot.

Hillsman had been there before, though. It had even been the same TV station, WCCO-TV, that had first called Wellstone's amazing victory eight years before.

Hillsman turned to Jesse. "They're usually not wrong on these things, Jesse," he said. "But if it's going to make you feel more comfortable, we could wait for a second checkmark if you want to."

Then an independent TV station—KMSP—put up the next checkmark. Jesse looked at Hillsman.

"Ooohh, that's only really half a checkmark," Hillsman said, since KMSP didn't have the network resources the larger stations had.

But then NBC called it. Then ABC.

"Jesse," Hillsman said, "you trusted me with the ads, right? You have to trust me now. You're the governor."

NBC's Maria Shriver—Schwarzenegger's wife—called on the Venturas' cell phone and made Jesse promise to give NBC his first national interview as governor.

State troopers showed up—they were now in charge of Jesse's safety.

It had to be true, Jesse thought.

Jesse finally took to the stage.

"First of all, and I say this very sincere: Thank you," Jesse said. "Thank you for renewing my faith that the American dream still lives.

"You know, it was back in '64 that a hero and an idol of mine beat Sonny Liston . . . he shocked the world. No one said he could do it. In later years, I think it was 1980, we sent a hockey team to the Olympics, a bunch of amateur kids who weren't given a chance. They had to face to Russians who were, like, professionals. Nobody gave them a chance and what happened? They shocked the world. Well now it's 1998 and the Americans dream lives on in Minnesota 'cause we SHOCKED THE WORLD!"

The crowd exploded in celebration. "Jes-SEE! Jes-SEE! Jes-SEE!"

"I believe it was 1981 that Adrian and I first sold out the civic center in St. Paul and you're still cheering me," Jesse said. "Only in '81 it was 'Jesse sucks.'"

"This is the great thing about America," he added. "The word 'can't' doesn't enter into your vocabulary. 'Can' does."

Watching his former student say those words on TV, "Mac" McInroy smiled. There was no question where Jesse had first heard that phrase—Mac and the other football coaches used to recite it, and other, similar inspirational sayings, to the players while they were doing jumping jacks and other calisthetics.

"We'd used that hundreds of times on every team that I ever coached," Mac recalls. He watched Jesse all night, but it wasn't until he said that "can't" wasn't in his vocabulary that Mac, in the comfort of his living room, wept.

"And then I cheered like hell," he says.

"MINneSOHta leads the way," Jesse went on. "Hopefully the Democrats and the Republicans will take notice now. . . . They will stop their partisan party politics and started doing what's right for the people . . .

"I didn't make a lotta promises," he continued. "I'm gonna do the best job that I can do. I'm human. I'll probably make mistakes. And let's remember that we all make 'em. And if they're mistakes from the heart, then you don't have to apologize for them."

Jesse thanked Friedline, treasurer Maline, spokeswoman Drewery, Webmaster Madsen, and others. He thanked Dean Barkley "for runnning two times and getting us major party status."

Out in the audience, Sue Barkley was almost overcome with sadness. It should be Dean up there, she thought. It should be Dean in the limelight, Dean earning the applause and cheers, Dean going to the Governor's Mansion.

But it wasn't. It was Jesse. Sue liked Jesse. She was happy for him. He was gracious and friendly, always mentioning Dean whenever he could, thanking him for everything he'd done to pave the way. But no one listened. That night, some kid next to her hadn't even known who Dean was, for godssakes. Had never even *heard* of him! Was this why her life had been turned upside down? For Jesse's benefit? Was this the reward for the years of mockery? For the second mortgage on the house?

So on election night '98, Sue's thoughts were bittersweet. Her family had undergone a great deal for what a lot of people—including her—thought was just damn foolishness. But instead of folly, November '98 brought her husband affirmation, and she was happy. "Without Dean, none of this would have happened," she says. "If Dean hadn't run three years in a row to keep the Reform Party as a major party it never would have happened."

Still, she would be lying if she claimed that she was jubilant that night. She looked at Jesse, who was basking in the glow of his victory, then she looked at her husband, in the shadows. She thought of their second mortgage, and the unfulfilled promises people made to help them pay it off, and her kids handing out leaflets in '92 and '94 and '96, and thought to herself as she gazed at her husband, "Oh, why can't this be you?"

She grabbed ahold of Dean and said as much. "I want everybody to know that you're the reason this is all happening," she said.

Dean said they knew, but Sue had her doubts.

"It did bother me," she says, "but eventually everybody will know or understand.

"And I guess what's most important is that Dean knows."

Then Jesse thanked Ty and Jade and Terry—"who about a year ago said to me, 'Are you *nuts?*!'"

Terry was having trouble believing any of this. In the back room, right after the networks put checkmarks next to her husband's name, she crawled into her mother's lap and cried.

She didn't know how to handle this. She was totally unprepared. She was happy for her husband, but what on earth was going to happen to them? To their family? And how on earth could she ever be able to carry off being a First Lady? She wore leather and jeans—she didn't think she'd be able to do it.

Jesse thanked Terry's parents and then, his voice trembling, he thanked his own. "They're not far from here, they're in Fort Snelling, but thank you," he said. By request, Jesse never mentioned his brother Jan, a very private man who now worked as a member of the Army Corps of Engineers.

He thanked Mae Schunk.

He still didn't believe it. He warned the crowd that maybe it wasn't really true. "I want you to remember something now though," he cautioned. "These are still numbers and we haven't received phone calls yet . . . that's the thing that has to happen . . . I took a lot of guff over my career in pro wrestling, but the one thing I learned is you gotta know how to lose before you can know how to win."

He was, in fact, more surprised than anybody. Just days before he had talked about getting back on his radio show.

Stunned, he didn't know what else to say. "You know what the nice thing about this gathering is? I don't have to answer any questions."

"How do you feel?" someone called out.

"How do I feel?" he responded. "It's still kind of numb, you know? It probably won't set in for another twenty-four hours or so. . . ."

Finally, he told the crowd to "party on!" and then he and Terry went back to the holding room where they could be alone, and Jesse could take a moment just to make sure this was really happening.

Coleman and Humphrey were also shocked. "If before the election somebody had told me that I would beat Skip by 130,000 votes. . . . but still not be the governor, I would have said he was crazy," Coleman says. "But the guy we thought we had to beat didn't turn out to be the right guy."

At Humphrey for Governor headquarters, Skip was depressed. He took the news very hard. Within a few weeks, he would announce that he was leaving Minnesota, at least temporarily, to teach at Harvard University's Kennedy School.

Out in the rest of the world, others from Jesse's past were just as incredulous.

In Los Angeles: "Jesse 'The Body' Ventura won for governor?" asked Elizabeth Burch, the casting agent who'd put Jesse in *Predator*. She called up Jesse's agent, Barry Bloom. "Is that our Jesse?!" she asked.

In Westchester County, New York: "Well, that's a weirdo," said "Classy" Fred Blassie. Blassie says that he "felt sorry for the people of Minnesota. He doesn't know anything about running a state or anything. How the hell's he gonna do anything?"

In Toronto, Damian Lee, writer and director of

Abraxas, Guardian of the Universe, laughed. "Outrageous!" he said.

In Sarasota, Florida, Okerlund was stunned. His attorney's daughter called him from Canterbury Park and put Jesse on the phone.

"You didn't think I could do it, didja Mean Gene?" Jesse asked.

Except for a brief spell when Jesse arranged a meeting with outgoing Governor Arne Carlson for first thing in the morning, he and Terry and his friends and family and supporters partied on and on.

In the wee hours, the final returns came in. Jesse had won 37% of the vote, or 768,356 votes. Coleman was second, with 35% or 713,410. Humphrey garnered just 28% or 581,497.

At five AM or so, the troopers shuttled Jesse and Terry into a state-owned Lincoln and whisked them into a hotel 500 or so yards away. Though she was terrified, Terry'd had the presence of mind to bring along some champagne. They popped the cork, had a swig, and smiled at each other.

"You're the Governor!" Terry squealed.

"And you're the First Lady," Jesse said, smiling.

In a few hours, the city and the state and the known universe would awake from its slumber to the news of Jesse's victory. Jesse and Terry were just minutes away from their lives being turned inside out and upside down; things would never be the same. But, at least for that moment, their lives were still their own.

Governor Jesse Ventura awoke early on November 4 and sped off to do a satellite interview with *CBS This Morning.*

"Bear with me," he told the co-host. "I'm on no sleep, so don't ask me too hard of questions today."

He'd sworn to Terry that he was going to stay the same old Jesse. That night, he might have stood at the sidelines with the Champlin Park High School football team. But most of his post-election activities weren't so down-to-earth.

He began his tour into the land of the fabulous, appearing in a pinstriped suit—looking very gubernatorial—as a guest on the *Tonight Show with Jay Leno,* sandwiched between comedian Garry Shandling and supermodel Stephanie Seymour.

"Have you seen my wife?" Jesse quipped. "I don't need to look for an intern, rest assured."

Everybody wanted a piece of him, from *The Late, Late Show with Tom Snyder,* to *Meet the Press with Tim Russert* ("If I call you Jesse 'The Mind' Ventura, will you call me Tim 'The Body' Russert?" the rotund newsman asked as a final question. "Take off your shirt right now, Tim," Jesse said. "Let's see what you got.") He was supposed to be on the cover of *Time,* but that got squashed when House Speaker Gingrich resigned.

His "campaign slogans" made David Letterman's Top Ten List, a zeitgeist indicator if there ever was one. ("No. 10—He's already used to deceiving the public . . . No. 7—A man in tights has nothing to hide . . . No. 3—Combining the wise economic stewardship of Hulk Hogan and the progressive policies of Jimmy 'Superfly' Snuka . . . No. 1—It's the stupidity, stupid.") Even President Clinton weighed in, nothing that in the wake of Jesse's victory, "A lot of politicians are going to be spending time in gyms now."

As the muck of scandal continued to drown Washington, D.C., there was even talk of Jesse himself running for President some day, though Jesse shrugged off that noise. He'd taken Coleman to task for running for governor so soon after running for mayor, he would say, so for him to do the same thing—albeit on a much larger scale—would be hypocritical. More realistically, Jesse must have known he was in way over his head as governor. The idea of being President was, at least for now, insane.

His was one of the biggest stories of the year. In the next few months, Jesse would earn a slot as a subject on A&E's *Biography, Dateline NBC*, and myriad others. In a way, it kind of pissed Jesse off—everybody was making money off of him except for him.

Particularly irritating was Vince Jr. Though Vince and Jesse had a tumultuous past, the Connecticut-based businessman was no fool. He talked about Jesse on NBC's *Today* show and issued a press release wishing Jesse good luck from his "former boss for seven years."

"As a former WWF Superstar," Vince Jr. said, Jesse "has what it takes to survive in any area—be it politics or sports entertainment." He made sure to note that "Americans can still look back at Jesse's most famous ring battles with World Wrestling Federation Superstars, his outrageous antics, his trademark flamboyant announcing and outlandish costumes on video with the release of *Jesse "The Body" Ventura: The Mouth, The Myth, The Legend* for $14.95, available at major retail stores."

Department stores were flooded with Jesse-themed T-shirts. "Our governor can beat up your governor" being only the most notable of a wide selection. Jesse decided that he'd be a fool not to get a little piece of the action. It was, after all, his moment. Why should leeches like Vince Jr. make all the money?

One year before, Jesse had been trying to shop his autobiography around, but no publisher had shown an

iota of interest. Now, with a huge political upset that
was international news, his life story was more mar-
ketable. A few publishers passed on the project, but it
was soon auctioned off by a Los Angeles-based agent
to Villard for somewhere in the neighborhood of
$500,000.

Immediately the media criticized him for his side
venture. Jesse didn't see the big deal.

"First of all, that's how I earned a living before I
became a governor," he said. "Second of all, I'm not
collecting a dime right now of government money.
I've been unemployed since July 21 because of our
great FCC laws. Where I have to leave my job in the
private sector while two career politicians can run
around and campaign and get paid by my tax dollars
while they're not doing their jobs that we elected them
to do. . . . I own the rights to my name. It's copy-
righted. I've done it before. If I want to sell my
name—Jesse 'The Body' Ventura—to advertising, I
think that I have every right to do so."

There was such a demand for the "Jesse Ventura
action figure," in fact, a company was hired to man-
ufacture them for sale—possible as a way to raise
campaign funds. Jesse's critics said that it was un-
seemly.

"Some people might say that it turns politics into
a kind of hucksterism," said MSNBC's John Hockenberry. But that cracked Jesse up.

"Waitaminute!" he said. "After what's happened
in Washington you're gonna accuse me of being a
huckster?!"

"I take your point," Hockenberry responded, "but
selling products is not the business of governing, necessarily, is it?"

"No it's not," Jesse admitted, "but selling one's

soul isn't either, is it? Or should it be? I'd rather sell a product than my influence.''

Within a month, Jesse would float the idea that Terry should be paid a salary of at least $25,000 for being the state's First Lady. As with all of the other post-election controversies, there was another hue and outcry by the media and little response by the public. The media, Jesse thought. He really was starting to hate those people.

"The press giveth and the press taketh away," Norm Coleman says. Reporters and commentators continued to get under Jesse's skin. Unlike most politicians, Jesse let it show. Hockenberry, for instance, asked Jesse about Minnesota Public Radio's Garrison Keillor, who had been ribbing Jesse pretty savagely in his weekly comedy-and-music show, *Prairie Home Companion.*

"I used to work in radio where I had to go out and earn a living and get advertisers," Jesse said. "Garrison Keillor works for public radio, so he works at the public trough and is subsidized by the very politicians and government. So I can imagine that he would take shots at me in some manner, because he never really had to go out and earn a living . . . He probably is scared that I'm going to take away his funding source." A few weeks later, Jesse proposed that the state eliminate all funding for Minnesota Public Radio.

If it was unnecessary for Jesse to fire back at his critics—even a bit childish—it was just Jesse being Jesse. Navy SEAL, pro wrestler, sports announcer, and talk radio shock jock, he'd been fighting back and speaking his mind for almost thirty years. He wasn't going to change now.

Even in the immediate aftermath of his victory, on

his KFAN post-election day show, he lashed back at KSTP's Jason Lewis. "I've got news for you, buddy-boy, and I hope you're listening out there. . . .'cause you know who I'm talking to," Jesse said. "I'm renaming you now Mr. Minnesota Wrong . . . Well, Mr. Wrong, stick it where the sun don't shine."

"I probably had it coming," Lewis admits, while acknowledging how odd it was to have Jesse even mention him, much less with such venom. Still, Lewis says, as Jesse's Number One critic, "I got four years of job security."

Lewis will have no shortage of material. Immediately after his win, Jesse was a loose cannon. Anyone who'd stood in his path was fair game. Hulk Hogan was trying to capitalize on Jesse's media by announcing that he might run for president in 2000. "I don't take it serious at all," Jesse said. "He's still involved in wrestling. It's a gimmick for him in wrestling. The problem with Hogan is his ego. He's no doubt the most *famous* wrestler in the world; he's no doubt made the most *money* of any wrestler in the world, but the thing that eats away at him is that in one night, I became the most respected former wrestler in the world."

He was bluntly honest, interesting, childish, and warm. He took potshots, made the same joke over and over, controlled as much of his media coverage as he could.

On Veterans Day, 1998, Governor-elect Ventura visited the graves of his parents at Fort Snelling and then went to the Veteran's Administration Medical Center in Minneapolis. He shook hands with officers, joking that he—just an enlisted man—was in charge, a slightly altered version of the ribbing his sergeant dad used to give his lieutenant mom.

"Imagine the old E-4, SK-3, storekeeper third class, U.S. Navy. It's kind of fun to have the officers respect the enlisted guys," he said. "On behalf of all those enlisted guys out there, 'Hey we got an enlisted commander-in-chief.' "[62] He pledged to "do the best job I can do as governor of Minnesota to make sure nobody forgets the sacrifices the veterans made."

He then headed to Roosevelt High, where he'd had so much fun. The neighborhood had changed a lot—the school now had a large Somali population.

"Do not become reliant on the government," he told the kids. "We are bigger than the government, You as an individual are bigger than the government, and I implore you stand on your own two feet. . . . You don't need the government. There's plenty of ways to get through college. You're smart enough. I have confidence in you."

"Get as much out of these schools as you can right now, because they're free," he said. "At the point that you leave here, you will pay—you will have to earn your way the rest of the way."[63]

In terms of actual governing, Jesse knew enough to know that he didn't know anything about running a state. Dean and Doug wouldn't be enough—he needed experts for his administration and, of higher priority, for his transition team.

"I feel like Rodney Dangerfield," Governor Ventura said, revealing his obscurely lowbrow tastes. "It's time to go *Back to School*." He assembled a tripartisan team—Democrats, Republicans, Reform Party members—and was heralded for most of his selections. He greatly relied on the advice and former staff of retired Congressman Tim Penny, a moderate Democrat who'd resigned from the House in disgust with the political process. Jesse also brought his old producer, David Ruth, to join his communications staff.

Then came time to pick his Cabinet, and for this his selections were fairly traditional as well—predominantly white and mostly political insiders, including Finance Commissioner Pam Wheelock—previously an aide to Norm Coleman—and a number of Carlson bureaucrats whom Jesse re-appointed. Dean Barkley was appointed to head up the office of Minnesota Planning.

Sure, there were a few stumbles. Turned out that Jesse's selection for commissioner of the state's Department of Natural Resources, former Navy SEAL and hunting enthusiast Alan Horner, had violated a number of hunting and fishing regulations and had been ticketed accordingly. Horner withdrew his name from consideration after two high-ranking officials of the agency resigned in protest of Horner's attitude toward enforcing game and fish laws.

He survived the Horner debacle just fine; Jesse's palpable Teflon quality remained as strong as ever. After decrying his opponent's acceptance of PAC money for so long, for instance, Jesse allowed his people to begin hitting up many of Minnesota's top corporations to fund his transition team. He said that he didn't look at the list of donors. And he got away with it.

He was offered a private seat for a February 15 Rolling Stones concert, acceptance of which would have violated the state's strict gift ban legislation— which prohibits elected officials from accepting gifts worth more than $5. He circumvented this by declaring February 15 ''Rolling Stones Day,'' which would allow him to attend as official business. He got away with that, too.

Jesse was still a loose cannon. Not long after the

election, the AFL-CIO held a central committee meeting in Bloomington, and Jesse accepted its invitation to speak. Before the election, Jesse had lobbied hard for the union's endorsement, playing up his Screen Actor's Guild and other union memberships, and had been very upset when they opted for Skip instead. Instead of taking this opportunity to secure their support for the future—as the union was clearly doing with its invitation—Jesse "started ripping on them for not endorsing him," according to Harvey Rockwood, who was there. "He gave the AFL-CIO council hell . . . It was just this nasty scene. He's not the kind of guy to offer an olive branch. With him, it's get even."

"He really needs some handlers around him that can teach him restraint," says Rockwood. "But that's gonna be really hard, since he didn't get where he was by using restraint . . . I don't think he sees any reason to change."

Clearly not. Jesse is who he is, and if you don't like it, tough shit. The Minnesota Chamber of Commerce held its convention and invited Jesse to speak to them as well. Business leaders awaited his speech eagerly, hoping he would address his proposal to cut taxes. Instead, Jesse announced that he wanted to repeal the $50 surcharge on Wave Runners. The crowd didn't know how to take it. A few of them even laughed. In the next few weeks, Jesse would propose even more legislation that affected him personally, including a bill to reduce the extra tax he had to pay on his Porsche.

Eventually, however, he made an attempt to fulfill his major campaign promise. After waffling for weeks, he finally proposed a tax rebate that would average $779 per family. The check was in the mail, he said. There would almost definitely be technical difficulties in his future. Sixty-three percent of the state had not voted for Jesse, it was constantly pointed out, and not one member of the Minnesota legislature was from the Reform Party, so he had no natural allies for any legislative proposal. "There will be a number of promises that he made that he can't deliver on,"[64] said state senate majority leader Roger Moe, Humphrey's LG candidate.

Generally, however, Jesse's first weeks in his new role went fairly well, and were very . . . well, very Jesse. He announced that his official car would be a sport-utility vehicle instead of the traditional luxury sedan. It would have extra-strong shocks, he said, "for running over reporters."

In early January, Jesse held "The People's Celebration," a sold-out event for 13,000 supporters—featuring blues guitarist Jonny Lang, as he had promised election night. Also making appearances were Warren Zevon (of "Send Lawyers, Guns, and Money" fame, from his first speech as a pissed-off Brooklyn Park resident); the band America (singing "Ventura Highway," of course, and "Horse with No Name" dedicated to Terry); and Jesse dressed in a Jimi Hendrix T-shirt, sunglasses, a bandanna, and three earrings. He was surprisingly reticent, delivering opening remarks consisting only of: "Yeah! THE BODY'S back for tonight! Thank you, everyone. LET'S PARTY!"

(He wasn't so merciful when Zevon called him onto the stage to sing a special version of "Werewolves of London": "Who put a flying head scissors kick on Hubert Humphrey?" Zevon asked. "Jesse The Body," screeched Jesse The Body. "Werewolf of MINnehSOHdah!")

•   •   •

The first weekend of 1999 was a typical Minnesota winter: a severe blizzard hit the area, icing the roads, stranding travelers, and inspiring a herd of cross-country skiers to hit local trails. The morning of Jesse's inaugural—Monday, January 4—Jesse woke to the coldest day in Minnesota in almost a year: temperatures dipped eleven below zero and, with the wind chill, hit fifty below in some areas.

"For a real man, the cold weather means nothing," said one of Jesse's inaugural guests, Arnold Schwarzenegger, to a reporter. "What means a lot to us is to celebrate with Jesse and Terry today."[65]

"Hold On, Change Is A Comin'," a gospel band sang at the beginning of the ceremony, held in the capital rotunda. A Navy Honor Guard entered and flanked the stage. After the national anthem, various others were sworn in—the attorney general, the state treasurer, Mae Schunk.

Finally, it was time for Jesse's first real starring role. Jesse was called to the stage. He looked even more humongous than usual in his black suit, an oversized boutonniere bursting from his right lapel.

Judge Paul Magnuson—who'd ruled that the WWF had to pay Jesse $895,526.86—presided, handing Terry the Bible to hold for her husband as he was sworn in. Jade and Ty stood behind him. He put his right hand in the air, his left on the Good Book, and solemnly recited his oath. When he was done, he turned and hugged his family.

After receiving an ovation, Jesse stepped up to the podium. Terry, Jade, and Ty slid back to their seats and gazed at him lovingly, as did Terry's parents, Gordon and Sharon Larson. Dean, Doug, Bill . . . everyone was there, including hundreds of citizens who had lined up to shake his hand.

"You know, I was down speaking in Austin, Minnesota, a week or so ago,'' Jesse said. ''A couple of weeks ago, to the Austin High School, and I asked them, you know, I'm assuming this office, and all during the campaign I never used a note. I never had a prepared speech ever, and I asked those high school kids in Austin, 'Should I change?' And they said 'Absolutely not.'

''They told me, 'We want to hear from your heart and we want to hear from your soul.' So that's what you're going to get today. I'm not changing . . .''

The audience clapped enthusiastically, Jade looking the happiest.

He thanked Judge Magnuson, Governor Carlson and his wife, other distinguished guests, his family, and the dozen or so Navy SEALs who had come. He thanked his mom and dad at Fort Snelling. ''I can tell right now, the ground is heating up a little bit where they're at,'' he said, ''because I think today, most of all, my mom and dad would look down and say 'I can't believe it. Look what he's done now.' ''

The eleven-minute speech was vintage Jesse. His promises were small, his allusions were to humble subjects: mom, dad, high-school football.

''And as I said on election night, certainly I'll make mistakes, but rest assured I will do the best job I possibly can, to the best of my ability. And I think that's all we ask of anyone in life: Do your best.

''I know when I coached football at Champlin Park High School, the young men that I work with there, I always tell them, 'I will never, ever, punish you for losing. But God help you if you quit on me.' Because there is a difference between losing and quitting. Someone will always lose. But if you quit, you can't go home and look at yourself in the mirror . . .

''But you know there's a lot of questions that go on.

'Is Jesse Ventura up for governing? Can Jesse Ventura do the job?' Well, I told you I was going to come here today and was going to speak from the heart. Well, not totally true. I have to read something . . .''

He reached inside his jacket pocket, and took out a letter. He put on his reading glasses.

"I received this yesterday and it says: 'I'm sure you must be nervous and apprehensive and maybe a little frightened by such a huge and challenging endeavor. But keep this in mind. You've been there. You've been pushed, tried and tested by the best. And you've passed with flying colors. Keep that hooyah spirit and don't change a thing.

" 'I wish you the very best of luck and success. Sincerely, Master Chief Terry "Mother" Moy.'

"So for any of you that have any doubts, he's standing to the left of me and I'll behave . . .''

Moy and two other SEALS—Dan Glasser and Bill Ranger—stood behind Jesse in full uniform. Combined with the others in the audience—including Dyer and Nelse—they totaled about a dozen men. To a man, they were filled with pride with Janos the Dirty.

". . . We must put down the partisan party politics and look at the bigger picture,'' Jesse said. "We must look at the picture of these young people who have now come on board, these young people who want to be part of the system, who want to vote and take part of the great thing we have here called the United States of America, and the state of Minnesota . . .

"So that's the challenge before us now. To keep these young people involved, to keep opening the arms of government and making it citizen-friendly . . . These were first-time voters . . . And one main thing came out. They said, 'Honesty. Honesty. That's what we want. Don't tell us what we necessarily want to hear. We want honesty.' And I tell you today, that the one thing you'll get from Governor Jesse Ventura—you may not always want to hear it—but you will get honesty . . .

". . . Remember this: We are all Minnesotans—that's the bottom line, whether you're a Democrat, a Republican, a Reform Party or whatever party you might be—we are all Minnesotans. Now we move forward to do Minnesota's business, and we will do it to the best of our ability."

He raised his right hand in a fist, and emitted the cheer that had got him through so many of his toughest challenges.

"Hooyah!" Jesse said.

ABOUT THE AUTHOR

As of March 1999, Jake Tapper is a Washington correspondent for *Salon Magazine*. His work has appeared in the *Washington Post, New York Times Magazine, George, Entertainment Weekly*, on National Public Radio's "All Things Considered,"and on the on-line humor 'zines *Timothy McSweeney's Internet Tendency* and *suck.com*. A magna cum laude and Phi Beta Kappa graduate of Dartmouth College, Tapper is contributing cartoonist for *Roll Call*, and his cartoons and caricatures have appeared in the *Washington Post, Philadelphia Inquirer*, and the *Los Angeles Times*. Raised in Philadelphia, he currently lives in Washington, D.C.

Notes

1. Britt Robson, *City Pages*, September 30, 1988.
2. Kevin Dockery and Bill Fawcett, eds., *The Teams: An Oral History of the U.S. Navy SEALs*, William Morrow and Company, 1998.
3. From *The Teams*.
4. David Hanners, St. Paul Pioneer Press, 1998.
5. Robson.
6. From *The Teams*.
7. Robson.
8. Robson.
9. Robson.
10. From *The Teams*.
11. Pam Belluck, *The New York Times*, November 4, 1998.
12. Robson.
13. Interview with Brian Lamb on C-SPAN, December 1998.
14. J. Mark Watson, "Outlaw Motorcyclists: An Outgrowth of Lower Class Cultural Concerns," in *Deviant Behavior: A Text-Reader in the Sociology of Deviance, Fifth Edition*, Delos H. Kelly, ed., (New York: St. Martin's Press, 1996).
15. Lamb.
16. Hanners.
17. Lawrence Linderman, *Penthouse*, March 1989.
18. Hanners.
19. Champ Thomas, *Inside Pro Wrestling*, USA Books, 1976.
20. Linderman.
21. von Sternberg, *Star Tribune*, August 25.
22. Linderman.
23. Linderman.
24. Deposition of Jesse Ventura in *Jesse Ventura* v. *Titan Sports Inc.*, taken on May 14, 1992.
25. Jim Jerome, *People*, May 24, 1982.
26. Hanners.
27. Deposition, 1992.
28. Sharon Mazer, *Professional Wrestling: Sport and Spectacle*, Jackson: University Press of Mississippi, 1998.
29. Linderman.
30. Judy Quinn, *Daily Variety*, December 1998.
31. Robson.
32. Robson.
33. Robson.
34. Gannett, February 27, 1992.

35. Lawrence Linderman, *Penthouse*, March 1989.
36. Ventura deposition, 1992.
37. Ventura deposition, 1992.
38. Deposition of Richard K. Glover, October 9, 1992.
    St Paul Pioneer Press, November 11.
39. "Four Years of Ventura-isms," Brooklyn Park *Sun Post*, January 4, 1995.
40. "Americans Take Sides," *Newsweek*, November 26, 1990.
41. Brooklyn Park *Sun Post*, March 31, 1993.
42. Greg Gordon, *Star Tribune*, November 11, 1998.
43. von Sternerg and Dane Smith, *Star Tribune*, October 23, 1998.
44. Kevin Duchschere, *Star Tribune*, August 2, 1994.
45. Duchschere.
46. Gannett *News Service*, February 27, 1992.
47. Glenn Sheeley, *The Atlanta Constitution*, September 9, 1991.
48. Rhonda Hillbery, *The Los Angeles Times*, November 2, 1991.
49. Dane Smith, *Star Tribune*, May 17, 1995.
50. Robson.
51. Lamb.
52. Cheryl Johnson, *Star Tribune*, December 16, 1997.
53. Robson.
54. G. Theodore Mitan, *Politics in Minnesota*, University of Minnesota Press, Minneapolis, 1970.
55. Donald Leavitt and Bruce Nord, "Minnesota: Changing Political Cultures," in *Perspectives on Minnesota, Government and Politics*, Millard L. Gieske and Edward R. Brandt, Eds., (Dubuque: Kendall/Hunt Publishing, 1977).
56. von Sternberg, *Star Tribune*, August 25, 1998.
57. Robson.
58. von Sternberg, *Star Tribune*, June 7, 1998.
59. von Sternberg and Smith.
60. von Sternberg and Smith.
61. C J, *Star Tribune*, November 17, 1998.
62. Jim Ragsdale, St. Paul *Pioneer Press*, November 12, 1998.
63. Ragsdale.
64. Associated Press.
65. Associated Press.